ADOLF HITLER

ADOLF HITLER

Dennis Wepman

1985
CHELSEA HOUSE PUBLISHERS
NEW YORK

SENIOR EDITOR: William P. Hansen
ASSOCIATE EDITORS: John Haney
　　　　　　　　　Richard Mandell
　　　　　　　　　Marian Taylor
EDITORIAL COORDINATOR: Karyn Gullen Browne
EDITORIAL STAFF: Jennifer Caldwell
　　　　　　　　Susan Quist
ART DIRECTOR: Susan Lusk
ART ASSISTANTS: Teresa Clark
　　　　　　　　Carol McDougall
　　　　　　　　Tenaz Mehta
LAYOUT: Irene Friedman
COVER DESIGN: Mike Stromberg
PICTURE RESEARCH: Susan Quist

First Printing

Library of Congress Cataloging in Publication Data

Wepman, Dennis.
　　Adolf Hitler.

　　(World leaders past & present)
　　Bibliography: p.
　　Includes index.
　　1. Hitler, Adolf, 1889–1945—Juvenile literature.
2. Heads of state—Germany—Biography—Juvenile literature.
[1. Hitler, Adolf, 1889–1945.　　2. Heads of state]
I. Title　　II. Series.
DD247.H5W43　1985　　943.086'092'4　[B]　85-3795
ISBN 0-87754-578-2

Chelsea House Publishers
Harold Steinberg, Chairman & Publisher
Susan Lusk, Vice President
A Division of Chelsea House Educational Communications, Inc.

Chelsea House Publishers
133 Christopher Street
New York, N.Y. 10014

Photos courtesy of AP/Wide World Photos, The Bettmann Archive, and
United Press International

Contents

CHELSEA HOUSE PUBLISHERS

WORLD LEADERS PAST & PRESENT

ADENAUER
ALEXANDER THE GREAT
MARK ANTONY
KING ARTHUR
KEMAL ATATÜRK
CLEMENT ATTLEE
BEGIN
BEN GURION
BISMARCK
LEON BLUM
BOLÍVAR
CESARE BORGIA
BRANDT
BREZHNEV
CAESAR
CALVIN
CASTRO
CATHERINE THE GREAT
CHARLEMAGNE
CHIANG KAI-SHEK
CHOU EN-LAI
CHURCHILL
CLEMENCEAU
CLEOPATRA
CORTEZ
CROMWELL
DANTON
DE GAULLE
DE VALERA
DISRAELI
EISENHOWER
ELEANOR OF AQUITAINE
QUEEN ELIZABETH I
FERDINAND AND ISABELLA

FRANCO
FREDERICK THE GREAT
INDIRA GANDHI
GANDHI
GARIBALDI
GENGHIS KHAN
GLADSTONE
HAMMARSKJÖLD
HENRY VIII
HENRY OF NAVARRE
HINDENBURG
HITLER
HO CHI MINH
KING HUSSEIN
IVAN THE TERRIBLE
ANDREW JACKSON
JEFFERSON
JOAN OF ARC
POPE JOHN XXIII
LYNDON JOHNSON
BENITO JUÁREZ
JFK
KENYATTA
KHOMEINI
KHRUSHCHEV
MARTIN LUTHER KING
KISSINGER
LENIN
LINCOLN
LLOYD GEORGE
LOUIS XIV
LUTHER
JUDAS MACCABEUS

MAO
MARY, QUEEN OF SCOTS
GOLDA MEIR
METTERNICH
MUSSOLINI
NAPOLEON
NASSER
NEHRU
NERO
NICHOLAS II
NIXON
NKRUMAH
PERICLES
PERÓN
QADDAFI
ROBESPIERRE
ELEANOR ROOSEVELT
FDR
THEODORE ROOSEVELT
SADAT
SUN YAT-SEN
STALIN
TAMERLAINE
THATCHER
TITO
TROTSKY
TRUDEAU
TRUMAN
QUEEN VICTORIA
WASHINGTON
CHAIM WEIZMANN
WOODROW WILSON
XERXES

Further titles in preparation

ON LEADERSHIP
Arthur M. Schlesinger, jr.

LEADERSHIP, it may be said, is really what makes the world go round. Love no doubt smooths the passage; but love is a private transaction between consenting adults. Leadership is a public transaction with history. The idea of leadership affirms the capacity of individuals to move, inspire and mobilize masses of people so that they act together in pursuit of an end. Sometimes leadership serves good purposes, sometimes bad; but whether the end is benign or evil, great leaders are those men and women who leave their personal stamp on history.

Now, the very concept of leadership implies the proposition that individuals can make a difference. This proposition has never been universally accepted. From classical times to the present day, eminent thinkers have regarded individuals as no more than the agents and pawns of larger forces, whether the gods and goddesses of the ancient world or, in the modern era, race, class, nation, the dialectic, the will of the people, the spirit of the times, history itself. Against such forces, the individual dwindles into insignificance.

So contends the thesis of historical determinism. Tolstoy's great novel *War and Peace* offers a famous statement of the case. Why, Tolstoy asked, did millions of men in the Napoleonic wars, denying their human feelings and their common sense, move back and forth across Europe slaughtering their fellows? "The war," Tolstoy answered, "was bound to happen simply because it was bound to happen." All prior history predetermined it. As for leaders, they, Tolstoy said, "are but the labels that serve to give a name to an end and, like labels, they have the least possible connection with the event." The greater the leader, "the more conspicuous the inevitability and the predestination of every act he commits." The leader, said Tolstoy, is "the slave of history."

Determinism takes many forms. Marxism is the determinism of class, Nazism the determinism of race. But the idea of men and women as the slaves of history runs athwart the deepest human instincts. Rigid determinism abolishes the idea of human freedom—the assumption of free choice that underlies every move we make, every word we speak, every thought we think. It abolishes the idea of human responsibility, since it is manifestly unfair to reward or punish people for actions that are by definition beyond their control. No one can live consistently by any deterministic creed. The Marxist states prove this themselves by their extreme susceptibility to the cult of leadership.

More than that, history refutes the idea that individuals make no difference. In December 1931 a British politician crossing Park Avenue in New York City between 76th and 77th Streets around ten-thirty at night looked in the wrong direction and was knocked down by an automobile—a moment, he later recalled, of a man aghast, a world aglare: "I do not understand why I was not broken like an eggshell or squashed like a gooseberry." Fourteen months later an American politician, sitting in an open car in Miami, Florida, was fired on by an assassin; the man beside him was hit. Those who believe that individuals make no difference to history might well ponder whether the next two decades would have been the same had Mario Contasini's car killed Winston Churchill in 1931 and Giuseppe Zangara's bullet killed Franklin Roosevelt in 1933. Suppose, in addition, that Adolf Hitler had been killed in the street fighting during the Munich *Putsch* of 1923 and that Lenin had died of typhus during the First World War. What would the 20th century be like now?

For better or for worse, individuals do make a difference. "The notion that a people can run itself and its affairs anonymously," wrote the philosopher William James, "is now well known to be the silliest of absurdities. Mankind does nothing save through initiatives on the part of inventors, great or small, and imitation by the rest of us—these are the sole factors in human progress. Individuals of genius show the way, and set the patterns, which common people then adopt and follow."

Leadership, James suggests, means leadership in thought as well as in action. In the long run, leaders in thought may well make the greater difference to the world. But, as Woodrow Wilson once said, "Those only are leaders of men, in the general eye, who lead in action. . . . It is at their hands that new thought gets its translation into the crude language of deeds." Leaders in thought often invent in solitude and obscurity, leaving to later generations the tasks of imitation. Leaders in action—the leaders portrayed in this series—have to be effective in their own time.

And they cannot be effective by themselves. They must act in response to the rhythms of their age. Their genius must be adapted, in a phrase of William James's, "to the receptivities of the moment." Leaders are useless without followers. "There goes the mob," said the French politician hearing a clamor in the streets. "I am their leader. I must follow them." Great leaders turn the inchoate emotions of the mob to purposes of their own. They seize on the opportunities of their time, the hopes, fears, frustrations, crises, potentialities.

They succeed when events have prepared the way for them, when the community is waiting to be aroused, when they can provide the clarifying and organizing ideas. Leadership ignites the circuit between the individual and the mass and thereby alters history.

It may alter history for better or for worse. Leaders have been responsible for the most extravagant follies and most monstrous crimes that have beset suffering humanity. They have also been vital in such gains as humanity has made in individual freedom, religious and racial tolerance, social justice and respect for human rights.

There is no sure way to tell in advance who is going to lead for good and who for evil. But a glance at the gallery of men and women in *World Leaders—Past and Present* suggests some useful tests.

One test is this: do leaders lead by force or by persuasion? By command or by consent? Through most of history leadership was exercised by the divine right of authority. The duty of followers was to defer and to obey. "Theirs not to reason why,/ Theirs but to do and die." On occasion, as with the so-called "enlightened despots" of the 18th century in Europe, absolutist leadership was animated by humane purposes. More often, absolutism nourished the passion for domination, land, gold and conquest and resulted in tyranny.

The great revolution of modern times has been the revolution of equality. The idea that all people should be equal in their legal condition has undermined the old structures of authority, hierarchy and deference. The revolution of equality has had two contrary effects on the nature of leadership. For equality, as Alexis de Tocqueville pointed out in his great study *Democracy in America*, might mean equality in servitude as well as equality in freedom.

"I know of only two methods of establishing equality in the political world," Tocqueville wrote. "Rights must be given to every citizen, or none at all to anyone . . . save one, who is the master of all." There was no middle ground "between the sovereignty of all and the absolute power of one man." In his astonishing prediction of 20th-century totalitarian dictatorship, Tocqueville explained how the revolution of equality could lead to the "*Führerprinzip*" and more terrible absolutism than the world had ever known.

But when rights are given to every citizen and the sovereignty of all is established, the problem of leadership takes a new form, becomes more exacting than ever before. It is easy to issue commands and enforce them by the rope and the stake, the concentration camp and the *gulag*. It is much harder to use argument and achievement to overcome opposition and win consent. The Founding Fathers of the United States understood the difficulty. They believed that history had given them the opportunity to decide, as

Alexander Hamilton wrote in the first Federalist Paper, whether men are indeed capable of basing government on "reflection and choice, or whether they are forever destined to depend . . . on accident and force."

Government by reflection and choice called for a new style of leadership and a new quality of followership. It required leaders to be responsive to popular concerns, and it required followers to be active and informed participants in the process. Democracy does not eliminate emotion from politics; sometimes it fosters demagoguery; but it is confident that, as the greatest of democratic leaders put it, you cannot fool all of the people all of the time. It measures leadership by results and retires those who overreach or falter or fail.

It is true that in the long run despots are measured by results too. But they can postpone the day of judgment, sometimes indefinitely, and in the meantime they can do infinite harm. It is also true that democracy is no guarantee of virtue and intelligence in government, for the voice of the people is not necessarily the voice of God. But democracy, by assuring the rights of opposition, offers built-in resistance to the evils inherent in absolutism. As the theologian Reinhold Niebuhr summed it up, "Man's capacity for justice makes democracy possible, but man's inclination to injustice makes democracy necessary."

A second test for leadership is the end for which power is sought. When leaders have as their goal the supremacy of a master race or the promotion of totalitarian revolution or the acquisition and exploitation of colonies or the protection of greed and privilege or the preservation of personal power, it is likely that their leadership will do little to advance the cause of humanity. When their goal is the abolition of slavery, the liberation of women, the enlargement of opportunity for the poor and powerless, the extension of equal rights to racial minorities, the defense of the freedoms of expression and opposition, it is likely that their leadership will increase the sum of human liberty and welfare.

Leaders have done great harm to the world. They have also conferred great benefits. You will find both sorts in this series. Even "good" leaders must be regarded with a certain wariness. Leaders are not demigods; they put on their trousers one leg after another just like ordinary mortals. No leader is infallible, and every leader needs to be reminded of this at regular intervals. Irreverence irritates leaders but is their salvation. Unquestioning submission corrupts leaders and demeans followers. Making a cult of a leader is always a mistake. Fortunately hero worship generates its own antidote. "Every hero," said Emerson, "becomes a bore at last."

The signal benefit the great leaders confer is to embolden the rest of us to live according to our own best selves, to be active, insistent, and resolute in affirming our own sense of things. For great leaders attest to the reality of human freedom against the supposed inevitabilities of history. And they attest to the wisdom and power that may lie within the most unlikely of us, which is why Abraham Lincoln remains the supreme example of great leadership. A great leader, said Emerson, exhibits new possibilities to all humanity. "We feed on genius. . . . Great men exist that there may be greater men."

Great leaders, in short, justify themselves by emancipating and empowering their followers. So humanity struggles to master its destiny, remembering with Alexis de Tocqueville: "It is true that around every man a fatal circle is traced beyond which he cannot pass; but within the wide verge of that circle he is powerful and free; as it is with man, so with communities."

New York

1

The Child

In September 1908 a shabby young man walked into the magnificent building of the Vienna Academy of Fine Arts to apply for admission. He wore an old black overcoat, many sizes too large for him, the gift of a used-clothes merchant. An awkward, small-town boy with a ninth-grade education, he was naturally nervous—especially so because he had already tried to enter this prestigious school the year before and failed.

He knew that admissions standards were high. Of the 112 applicants who had tried to get in the previous fall, only 27 had been accepted. The young man had done the best he could, and passed the first part of the test. He was not a bad artist, as his surviving pictures prove, but he never did anything original or showed any creative imagination. He could copy photographs or other pictures and did architecturally accurate drawings of public buildings in Vienna. However, in 1907 his test drawings had been graded "unsatisfactory." They were criticized not only for not including enough human figures but also for failing to portray such figures in correct proportion.

After this initial setback he worked diligently to improve his art and even took private drawing lessons. Much depended on his getting into school.

Adolf Hitler painted this watercolor of a Vienna church, the Karlskirche, when he was in his early 20s. Fond of drawing from early childhood, the future dictator very often sketched secretly in school when he was supposed to be studying.

A pen-and-ink drawing of Hitler at age 16, made by a schoolmate. With his uncombed hair, tiny mustache, and dreamy eyes, he looked more like a poet than the devoted militarist he was soon to become.

13

Klara, Hitler's mother, was a study in contrasts to her brutal, hard-drinking husband. Gentle and affectionate, she was adored by her son. He was devastated by her death when he was 18.

He had told his family back home in the small town of Urfahr that he was a student at the Vienna Academy, and he was living on an orphan's state pension, to which he was entitled only if he was a full-time student. He needed something to justify his life in Vienna.

He fared even worse on his second application. The dean was so little impressed by the new drawings that he would not allow the boy to take the written part of the test. He suggested that the young man apply to the School of Architecture and try to become an architectural draftsman, since he liked to draw buildings. In any case, he told him, "You will never be a painter."

Unfortunately, the School of Architecture was closed to him too. He could not enter a technical school at that level without an *abitur*, the equivalent of a high school diploma. But the boy had dropped out of school after only the ninth grade.

It seemed to him he had reached a dead end. Prevented by the social system from preparing himself for a career as an artist, the young man could see no escape from a life of poverty and the dull routine of a laborer. During the next 35 years this angry and frustrated character never forgot the blow he received in the dean's office that autumn day. Adolf Hitler bore a grudge against educational élitism even after he became chancellor of Germany and head of one of the most powerful countries in the world. Some historians, with hindsight as an ally, contend that the rejection was a factor in his eventual attempt to remake German culture according to his own tastes and ideals. It most probably also contributed to the rabid anti-intellectualism which was to characterize his later life.

Historians like to speculate about what would have happened *if*. . . . Perhaps *if* that ill-dressed, poorly educated country boy with the pinched, hungry face had had a little more artistic talent. . . . Or *if* the dean of the Vienna Academy of Fine Arts had been a little less critical, the world might have been spared the nightmare into which this frustrated young man was eventually to plunge it.

Looking back on that period of Hitler's life, it is

hard to fathom the reasons for the intensity of his bitterness. Although his own writing about his youth presents a picture of cruel poverty and humiliation, the evidence now available shows that he had a fairly conventional Austrian upbringing. His adolescence gave little indication of the shattering effect he was to have on the world.

If there was nothing too extraordinary or tragic in Hitler's family background, there were, however, some dark elements that left their marks on him. His father, Alois Hitler, was the illegitimate son of Anna Schicklgrüber, who later married an unemployed miller named Hiedler. The identity of Adolf's paternal grandfather has never been definitely established, but Alois took his stepfather's name, which he spelled Hitler.

The name Hitler is not German, but probably a variant of the Czechoslovakian names Hidlar or Hidlarcek. It appears with many spellings—Huttler, Hydler, Hiettler, Hittler, etc.—in the records of that region from the 15th century, always the family name of poor farmers.

Alois was married three times, the last time to

Hitler's father, Alois, wears the uniform of his rank, a full inspector of customs. Respected as efficient, honest, and highly professional on the job, at home Alois was a harsh, tyrannical husband and father.

Members of the Hitler Youth movement burn "Jewish-Marxist" books in 1938. Book burnings, which were strongly encouraged by Hitler's violently anti-intellectual, anti-Semitic regime, became a common sight in both Germany and Austria during the 1930s.

Klara Pölzl, 23 years his junior and the daughter of his first cousin. The family relationship was too close for them to be legally married in the Catholic Church, but they managed to get special permission from Rome, probably because Klara was already pregnant by Alois. It was from this marriage that Adolf Hitler was born in 1889.

According to most reports, Alois was a bully who ruled his family as despotically as he did the customs office in which he was a senior inspector. "An energetic champion of law and order," as his obituary notice described him, he demanded total obedience and terrorized everyone in the family—his children, his mousy little wife, even the dog, which he often whipped till it wet the floor. Adolf apparently feared and worshipped his father at the same time. With this model, it is not hard to see where he got his idea of masculinity. Brutal authoritarianism became his ideal of German manhood.

Alois died—at an inn, with a glass of wine in his hand—when Adolf was 14. Under the constant nagging of his father, the boy had been a good student in the early grades, but even this paternal pressure had failed to keep him at his books by the time he reached age 12. And now, with no one to hound him about his bad grades, he was even less inclined to study. He had met with a conspicuous lack of academic success during the 1900–01 term and was clearly headed for further failure. He stayed on in school for two years after his father died, and then, at age 16, he quit.

Hitler spent a total of 10 years in school, and finished nine grades. In his last term, 1904–05, he failed mathematics and German and did well only in physical education and drawing. Obviously, higher learning would not be for him.

The people of the Austrian villages where he grew up remembered him as an independent boy, sullen in the face of authority, and generally a loner. The books he read were limited to adventure stories and military history. Upon reading them, he later wrote, "I seemed to experience the titanic battle in my innermost being."

Even when he played, the military streak in his

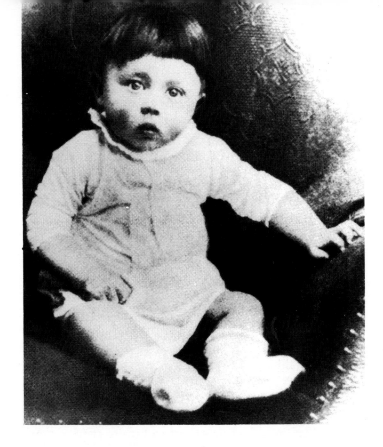

Adolf Hitler as a baby. As he grew up, he became what his sister later recalled as "a scrubby little rogue." Adolf's disrespectful attitude prompted frequent beatings from his father, who was an iron-handed disciplinarian.

character was apparent. The only games that appealed to Hitler as a child were war games, which he pursued until his comrades were exhausted. He himself was never a fighter, always a strategist. "He used his tongue instead of his fists," as one historian wrote. And he was always the leader.

One of his high school teachers remembered him clearly: "Willful, arrogant and irascible. . . . Moreover, he was lazy. . . . He reacted with ill-concealed hostility to advice or reproof; at the same time, he demanded of his fellow pupils their unqualified subservience."

The few pictures of the young Hitler that still exist seem to bear out this description. The solemn baby peering grimly at the camera, the haughty schoolboy standing a little aloof from his classmates, the sharp-featured, arrogant adolescent of 16—all of these faces perhaps reflect a person who sees himself as someone apart, that imagines himself somehow superior to others.

His mother, as the widow of a senior customs inspector, had a good pension, and she was indulgent to her only son. Adolf lived a pleasant, idle life at home for two years after leaving school, copying drawings and watercolors and dreaming of a career as an artist. Although he was close to his mother and his sister, Paula, he was now socially more of a loner than ever. He saw none of his former school-fellows and associated with none of his neighbors.

His only friend at this time was August Kubizek, the son of an upholsterer. Gustl, as Adolf called him, looked up to Hitler reverently. He was an ideal companion for young Adolf. He, too, had dropped out of school and, like Adolf, entertained artistic ambitions—he wanted to be a musician—but, more important, he was a born listener. And Hitler's natural gift for oratory had already begun to emerge. Gustl would listen to Adolf's outpourings for hours. "It was not what he said that first attracted me to him," Kubizek recalled many years later, "but how he said it."

Although life was easy for Adolf—he had a doting mother, an appreciative audience, and no responsibilities—he became restless. The family made their home in Linz, the capital of Upper Austria at that

Twelve-year-old Adolf Hitler (at top right) poses with his classmates in a 1901 school portrait. Hitler did poorly in high school, particularly in mathematics. His history teacher once referred to him as "willful, arrogant, and lazy."

In 1898, when Hitler was 9, his family moved to this house in Leonding, a village near Linz. Familiar only with country life until then, young Adolf was much impressed with Linz, which boasted a castle, churches, elegant buildings, and its own opera house.

time. It was the largest town he had ever lived in, but even there he felt stifled. A provincial capital could not provide him with the outlet that he felt his talents demanded. He was drawn to the big city—Vienna.

Vienna, the capital of Austria, was one of the most brilliant cities in Europe in the first decade of this century. It was the equal of Paris as a cultural center. Music, literature, and art flourished there, and after a few visits the young Hitler decided that it was the place for him. In 1907 he turned 18 and inherited his share of the money left by his father. He took it all out of the bank at once—700 kronen was enough with which to live comfortably for a year in Vienna at that time—and set out to become an art student at the famous Vienna Academy of Fine Arts.

2

The Dropout

Vienna was a hard school for me, but it taught me the most profound lesson of my life.
—ADOLF HITLER
writing in 1924 in *Mein Kampf*

Hitler's early days in Vienna were hardly glamorous. His life there began with failure and never rose much above that level.

When he was first refused admission to the academy, it was a great blow. "I was so sure of success," he wrote later, "that the news of my rejection took me completely by surprise, like a bolt from the blue." But fate had yet another disaster in store for young Adolf. A few months later, on December 21, 1907, his mother died.

Now he was really alone. Gustl Kubizek stayed with him in Vienna for a while, but Hitler seemed to have little capacity for personal relations. The academy's second rejection was the last straw. When his friend went back to Linz to visit his parents, Hitler disappeared without a trace, and Gustl returned to their room to find it empty.

The next five and a half years saw young Hitler grow increasingly isolated and eccentric. He had some money—more than he admitted to in his later writings—but he lived the life of a derelict, drifting aimlessly about in the great city. He slept in a variety of furnished rooms or in municipal shelters, living on bread and milk or what he could pick up at church soup kitchens. His health deteriorated. It was a dog-eat-dog world, and simply surviving was a terrible struggle.

Walpurgis Halle (Hall of the Spirits), a German mountain shrine built in the 1920s by a sect whose members believed in the gods of Germany's mythological past. Although he joined no such "religions," Hitler shared their passion for the glorious legends of Germany's Teutonic epoch.

Unemployed men congregate in Vienna in the 1920s. Hitler's firsthand experience as a Vienna derelict enabled him, a decade later, to speak with conviction to similarly impoverished and dissatisfied people.

Even after his meager orphan's pension stopped in 1911, Hitler never took a regular job. He scraped a living as a freelance artist, painting advertising posters or copying watercolor pictures of buildings to sell as postcards. When things were going especially badly, he found occasional employment as a laborer, shoveling snow or carrying baggage at the train station. As a last resort, he would ask for a little money from a maiden aunt in Linz.

He apparently made no friends during this period, and took no interest in women. When he actually did have some money, he simply stopped working until it was all spent. The other drifters who made his acquaintance in the city shelters remembered him as lazy and moody, but very serious. He never smoked or drank, and seemed to enjoy few pleasures.

His one entertainment was opera. He had no particular appreciation of music, but he loved the spectacle—especially the grandiose, melodramatic operas of Richard Wagner, which glorified Germany's mythological past.

The glory of Germany and the Germans came increasingly to preoccupy him, and politics became his favorite topic. Disappointed and frustrated in his own life, he lived more and more in the world of his imagination, where, for his own entertainment, he conjured up visions of a splendid and dramatic past. He dreamed of a simple time of clearly defined heroes and villains—just as it had been in the adventure books he had enjoyed as a child. The contrast between his own drab, impoverished existence and the lives of the glorious heroes of Wagner's operas only fueled his increasing anger and frustration. "He would fly into a temper at the slightest thing," his friend Gustl remembered from his first days in Vienna. "Wherever he looked, he saw injustice, hate, and enmity."

Vienna was just one of many European cities full of lonely, unhappy misfits like young Adolf Hitler. Such people tend to look for simple answers, and Vienna was full of exotic organizations whose members imagined they could solve the world's problems. There were astrologers and numerologists,

Devil worshippers and food faddists, religious fanatics and political extremists. It is not surprising that the solitary young man from Linz, with no friends, no trade, no money, and no prospects, was drawn to one of these groups.

One of the most prevalent views among the poor and hopeless in Vienna—and among many people of the middle and upper classes as well—was that the problems of Austria and Germany were due to racial mixing. Hitler was a regular reader of a popular Viennese magazine named *Ostara*, which argued persistently that the blond Germanic people (the Aryans as they were called then) were a "higher" race—a "Master Race" destined to rule the earth— and that all the problems of society resulted from the pollution of that race by inferior, darker peoples. The Gypsies, the Slavs, and especially the Jews were singled out as enemies of the ethnic purity of the Master Race.

Anti-Semitism—hatred of the Jews—had a long history in Austria. The mayor of Vienna during Hitler's years there was an outspoken anti-Semite. In fact, it was a common prejudice in those days, especially among those who considered themselves members of "polite society" and paragons of respectability. Anti-Semitism became one of Hitler's obsessions, a convenient explanation for the injustices he believed he had suffered.

A watercolor by Adolf Hitler. When he lived in Vienna from 1907 to 1913, Hitler made ends meet by painstakingly making postcard-size copies of paintings and selling them in taverns. Although his politics grew increasingly radical, his painting style remained highly orthodox.

Although at this time Hitler would talk politics by the hour to anyone who would listen, and tended to become particularly hysterical when discussing the glorious destiny of the Germans and the terrible threat of the Jews and communists, he had not yet considered actively pursuing a political career. He still thought of himself as an aspiring artist awaiting recognition.

The government of Austria, however, saw him as just another unemployed young man, and one whose time had come to report for military service. He had failed to register in Linz, and had lost all contact with his family there. The government police had traced him to Vienna, but had not yet located him among the drifters in the municipal shelters. It was only a matter of time, though, and in 1913 the bitter young man decided he was ready to move on.

He later wrote that he was drawn to Munich, across the border in Germany, by its advanced artistic life and the hope of finding better career opportunities. Although he also claimed that he was "repelled by the conglomeration of races" in Vienna, and that he had always had a burning desire to live in "the Fatherland" of the German

Hitler adored Richard Wagner's thunderous operas, which included such heroic figures as Queen Brunhilde (with feathered helmet), the dragonslayer Siegfried (in sailing ship), the war god Wotan (in winged helmet), and the beautiful Valkyrie. Although Hitler sometimes went hungry, he often managed to go to the opera.

Unaware of the momentous role he was to play in world history, Archduke Franz Ferdinand of Austria (with his wife Sofie) makes a smiling public appearance in 1914. Soon afterward, the royal couple was assassinated, a disaster that triggered World War I.

people, it appears that his chief reason for going to Munich may have been simply to avoid military service in the Austrian army.

In any case, with all his worldly goods in a single small bag, Adolf Hitler slipped quietly across the border in May 1913, one month after his twenty-fourth birthday. During his five years in Vienna he had made no friends and had accumulated few pleasant memories. He had earned no money, learned no trade, and acquired no direction in life.

What life in Vienna had taught him became apparent only much later. He had learned to survive. Life at the bottom had hardened him and sharpened his eye for opportunity. Perhaps more important for the path his life would take was the fact that he had found a focus for his dissatisfaction and frustration and an excuse for his failure. Two popular Viennese ideas—anti-Semitism and German glory—were to shape his destiny and that of all Europe. He had no affection for the city, but he never denied the value of what he had received from it.

Life in Munich was little different for Hitler. He returned to the aimless round of furnished rooms and tried to peddle his drawings in bars. He held out for eight months until, in January 1914, the authorities finally tracked him down and arrested him as a draft-dodger.

But his years on the streets had made him shrewd about dealing with authority, and he managed to talk his way out of trouble. Instead of being de-

A crowd of nationalistic Berliners unites in a fervent rendition of *Deutschland Uber Alles* ("Germany Above All") in 1914. Germans of all political persuasions and economic classes enthusiastically welcomed the nation's declaration of war on Russia.

ported back to Linz and quite probably sent to jail, he was excused and permitted to report to Salzburg.

As it turned out, he need not have been so fearful of a confrontation with the draft board, since the army medical examiner in Salzburg found him unfit for service of any sort. The report stated that he was too weak and was unable to bear arms. Thus, the physical deterioration that he had suffered in Vienna and Munich actually proved to be advantageous.

Without a word to family or acquaintances, he at once left Austria again and returned to his furnished room in Munich and his life as a starving artist. As he had in Vienna, he read the newspapers avidly and poured out his political beliefs to anyone who would listen. He said he intended to enter an art school, but he made no real effort to do so. Life drifted along without change, and he continued to eke out a meager existence by selling his small, careful drawings and watercolors.

If Hitler's personal life showed no prospect of change, the world around him was about to encounter dislocation and disaster.

On June 28, 1914, six months after Hitler returned to Munich "unable to bear arms," Europe was shaken by the news that Archduke Franz Ferdinand, the heir to the throne of the Austro-Hungarian Empire, had been assassinated by a Serbian terrorist. One month later, to the day, Austria was at war with Serbia, and World War I had begun.

The rest of Europe quickly fell into line. Russia joined its Slavic ally Serbia, and within days Germany stepped in to support Austria. On August 1 a state of war was declared in Germany, and the whole continent seemed to welcome the prospect of conflict. The tensions that had been building up among rival powers (France, Germany, Britain, and Russia) had become unendurable, and it almost seemed that people had been waiting for something to trigger an outbreak and clear the air.

Hitler was ecstatic. After nearly six lonely years he saw a chance to escape a listless life of poverty and humiliation and become actively involved in something. A European war would transform everything, perhaps overthrow the social order that had kept him down, and even bring about the emergence of that great German state which he believed was the hope of the world. Ten years later, in characteristically excessive language, he described his emotion on hearing of the outbreak of war. In his personal testament, entitled *Mein Kampf* ("My Struggle"), he wrote: "Overcome with rapturous enthusiasm, I fell on my knees and thanked Heaven from an overflowing heart for granting me the good fortune of being allowed to live at this time."

A photograph that happened to catch Hitler on that day shows that he did not exaggerate his feelings. We can see the exultation in his face as he stands in the crowd and learns that war has been declared.

He did not want to fight for Austria—he had fled from Vienna to avoid it—but he was passionately loyal to the cause of Germany. Here was an opportunity to break the cycle of failure and futility and throw himself into a battle for German nationalism and the ancient glory of the Fatherland. Even though he was not required to report for military service—he had been declared unfit in Austria and was not yet a citizen of Germany—he seized the moment and volunteered for service in the German army.

Now that it was wartime, medical records were not checked too closely and physical examinations were almost casual. He was accepted without comment, and within a week he was Private Hitler of the 16th Bavarian Reserve Infantry Regiment.

3

The Soldier

Adolf Hitler was a good soldier. His political enemies later tried to prove that he was a coward, but the records show very clearly that he was a dedicated, loyal, and brave infantryman. He had a cause, after all, and no soldier fights as well as one who really believes in his mission.

He had been dreaming of war since he was a little boy playing soldier in Linz, and now his childhood dream had come true. One member of his regiment recalled how Hitler reacted when he was issued a rifle for the first time. "He looked at it with delight," his companion reported, "like a woman looking at her jewelry."

Because of his lower-class, southern Austrian accent and his lack of education, it was impossible for him to rise very high in the aristocratic Imperial German Army. In the four years of World War I he was promoted only to the rank of corporal. But he did receive recognition for his courage and devotion to duty, and was twice awarded the Iron Cross. "Hitler never let us down," an officer reported, adding that the young Austrian was "always volunteering for the worst jobs."

He earned the respect of both his fellow enlisted men and his officers, yet he remained a loner. He did not smoke, drink beer, or talk about women, as did the other soldiers. In fact, he went so far as to lecture them against such vices. "He is an odd

A penciled self-portrait of Adolf Hitler, made during World War I. Art critics have noted that, while the young Hitler's architectural paintings were surprisingly professional for an untrained artist, he had little talent for drawing human beings.

By 1919 Hitler had decided that his destiny lay in national politics. Despite the passion of his oratory at that time, however, there was little to indicate that he had the makings of a major national leader.

Hitler had not yet shaped his mustache into its trademark style when he posed for this wartime photograph with fellow soldiers and his beloved terrier.

character," one of the other men in his regiment commented, "and lives in his own world."

But he was not disliked, and his comrades considered him "a nice fellow," if a little remote. When a little terrier wandered into camp one day, Hitler won its affection and the dog became completely devoted to him.

Hitler was assigned the dangerous and responsible task of carrying messages to and from the front line of battle. As the regimental dispatch carrier, he was often under fire, and more than once saved the day by his fearless devotion to duty. In Belgium he once threw himself in front of his commanding officer to protect him from machine-gun fire. Miraculously, he remained unhurt. The next day, he left a tent only seconds before a British shell blew it up, killing most of those inside. Hitler was already beginning to get a reputation for leading a charmed life.

In all the excitement of battle, Hitler never lost

his sense of purpose. Unlike most soldiers, he knew exactly why he was fighting. His love of country, his desire to "purify" and cure it of what he saw as the disease of internationalism—these were the motives that drove him to deeds of great valor. He saw enemies not only in the field but everywhere. Foreigners and their influence on Germany were like a virus to him, corrupting the pure blood of the Master Race.

But the war was not going well for Germany, and, despite the heroism of thousands of ordinary soldiers just as dedicated as Hitler, battle after battle proved inconclusive. As Germany's military planners had foreseen, the Russians were not well prepared for the struggle; but the French and the British, Russia's allies, put up a much stronger fight than anticipated. Even Hitler's luck could not last forever. In October 1916, while fighting in France, he was wounded in the leg and sent back to Germany.

Hitler's perception of the situation in Munich only served to strengthen his already considerable prejudices. He became convinced that Germany's Jews and communists were undermining the country's war effort. He was disgusted and could not wait to return to the battlefield, his little dog, and the stink of high explosives. When someone asked him where his home was, he always answered, "the 16th Regiment."

By 1918 it was becoming clear that Germany had lost the war. The influx of vast numbers of fresh American troops into the Allied forces in 1917 had sounded the death knell for Germany's hopes of victory on the Western Front. The people were disillusioned and in Berlin 400,000 workers went on strike for peace. Soldiers like Hitler, furious at the lack of fighting spirit in their country, wanted to continue the conflict right to the bitter end, but they could not contend with both the enemy in the field and subversion from within their own society.

After returning to battle Hitler was finally put out of commission on October 14, 1918. A gas shell struck near him, and he was blinded. He

Hitler, who was temporarily blinded by mustard gas in Belgium, was released from the hospital at the close of World War I. His four years in the trenches deeply embittered him toward pacifists and forged a burning sense of loyalty toward the German nation.

regained his sight on November 9, just two days before the Germans signed an armistice that brought World War I to an end.

An empire had fallen. Public support for the government collapsed. Workers' groups staged revolts in city after city throughout Germany. When the administration ordered in troops to suppress these rebellions, the soldiers often joined the dissidents. At last, royalty and industrialists were swept away, the military dictatorship that had grown during the war disappeared, and Germany became a socialist republic.

Hitler returned to the new Germany more displaced than ever; he had lost his home with the 16th Regiment, and the terrier that had stayed at his side throughout most of the war had been stolen. An ex-soldier—even one who, like Hitler, had been decorated six times in the Great War—could not find a place in the new society very easily.

Although he had read widely, Hitler still could not write any better than the average high school student. He had no great talent as an artist, and his efforts at get-rich-quick schemes in Vienna showed that he had no special flair for business either. The obvious thing for him to do was stay in the army, and that is exactly what Hitler did.

In the confusion following the 1918 armistice, many different factions competed for control in Germany. Some conservatives called for the reinstatement of the imperial family, while at the other end of the political spectrum the communists wanted to follow the example set by events in Russia in 1917, when a revolution had overthrown the old monarchic order and established a socialist republic. Between these two extremes, the majority wanted a democratic republic. Widespread rioting erupted, and the government's mishandling of a tense situation in Berlin almost resulted in that city becoming communist.

On January 3, 1919, Germany's first postwar president, Social Democrat Friedrich Ebert, dismissed the chief of police, a known communist sympathizer. Faced with what they considered extreme provocation, the Berlin communists called for immediate revolution, and 200,000 armed workers promptly took to the streets. Within a week, however, units of the Free Corps, whose members were rightist ex-soldiers like Hitler, had converged upon Berlin and brutally suppressed the rising. Two of the leading communists, Rosa Luxembourg (known as "Red Rosa") and her colleague Karl Liebknecht (who had been leading antiwar demonstrations and voicing his opposition to German militarism since 1913) were murdered by the Free Corps officers who had been ordered to escort them to prison.

Finally, later that same month, elections established a moderate representative government. Faced with the violence and instability that continued to plague Berlin, the new leaders chose the old cultural center of Weimar, in eastern Germany, as their capital.

The army's few remaining formations assumed responsibility for keeping the peace and stamping out the revolutionary movements that kept springing up among the poor and dissatisfied. Army spies in plain clothes sat in on meetings of leftist groups and reported anything that seemed particularly threatening. Hitler's passionate hatred of foreigners and communists made him a natural candidate for such employment, and he was assigned to the espionage section of an army regiment in Munich.

He was classed as an education officer, and his official job was to promote nationalism and discourage socialism among the soldiers. He organized meetings and gave talks on the aims of the government.

The general public discontent had given rise to dozens of radical political organizations. They sprang up like mushrooms in the fertile soil of Munich's poverty and confusion, and Hitler was sent to observe and report on them.

The various groups represented every shade of opinion. Most of them were ineffectual discussion societies—little more than social clubs—in which malcontents drank beer and let off steam. On September 12, 1919—a fateful day in history, as later

A Berlin workers' demonstration for peace. Postwar Germany was the scene of innumerable such rallies, many of which turned into bloody, uncontrollable riots.

Rosa Luxembourg was a leader of the Spartacists, a communist group that almost took over Berlin after World War I. The rebellious organization was annihilated by the rightist Free Corps, whose members also murdered "Red Rosa" and Karl Liebknecht, a close associate.

became apparent—Hitler was sent to investigate a group which called itself the German Workers party.

It was by no means an impressive gathering, and Hitler hardly thought it worth reporting. The party had been founded earlier that year by a toolmaker named Anton Drexler, and, despite its imposing name, contained only a handful of members. They met in small, cheap restaurants from time to time and argued about how to save the world. As might have been expected, their main points of agreement were entirely predictable: that the Germans were a Master Race destined to rule the world, that the Jews and the communists threatened their purity, and that something ought to be done. They wanted to "free" the workers from Marxism and prevent them from developing an international outlook, but beyond that they had no clear program, and no one took them any more seriously than any of the other fringe societies that filled the beer halls of Munich. Hitler spent the formal part of the meeting fighting off an understandable urge to sleep.

When the open discussion began, people got up to make their own points. Some of these points related to the topic of the meeting; others did not. Everyone had his own pet solution to the world's problems or his own complaint about the government. When Hitler heard one man urge that Bavaria declare independence and secede from Germany, he jumped to his feet to argue the point.

The unity of all Germanic people was one of Hitler's favorite themes. Only as a single people, he felt, could the Master Race rule the earth, and he argued the point with his usual passion. At his new job he had gained some experience of speaking to audiences, and his natural talent for oratory, last exercised on handfuls of derelicts in the municipal shelters of Vienna, had not deserted him. On this night he was especially eloquent, quite surpassing his previous outbursts. Before Hitler had finished, his opponent in the debate slunk away, at least according to Hitler's account, "like a wet poodle."

The committee of the German Workers party—all six of them—were impressed by this passionate

Speaking from the back of a truck, a German nationalist addresses an angry throng protesting the Treaty of Versailles, which ended both World War I and the German Empire. In 1919 such rallies could be seen on any street corner in the city of Berlin.

newcomer, and Drexler went up to shake his hand, give him a pamphlet, and urge him to come to the next meeting. Hitler accepted the pamphlet but declined the invitation.

The booklet interested Hitler more than he had anticipated, however, and when he received an invitation to a committee meeting of the German Workers party the following week, he accepted.

Some people considered Hitler's shrill, hysterical speaking style irritating, but Drexler recognized its hypnotic power. He knew he had found the most valuable asset of a political party, "a born popular speaker," and he invited Hitler to join.

Hitler, however, had his doubts. He could see that the insignificant little group did not amount to much and had no real program or internal structure. After a few days of hesitation, however, he decided to accept Drexler's invitation, reasoning that it would give him a chance to develop his own ideas and finally gain some practical experience in politics.

It was technically against the law for a member of the army to join a political party, but in this case there were exceptions to be made. The military, eager to rebuild Germany's shattered army, was looking to find, and possibly support, a movement with similar convictions. Hitler received orders to join the German Workers party.

Adolf Hitler had long believed that he was a man with a special destiny. His experience in the army had seemed to confirm it, and now there could be no doubt that his course was set. There would be no turning back.

4

The Agitator

Hitler was elected at once to the executive committee and put in charge of propaganda. Since the party was attracting neither attention nor money, Hitler decided to stake their whole treasury—the tiny sum of seven marks—on an advertisement for a mass meeting.

For a small organization like the German Workers party, the response was sensational. On October 16, 1919, a crowd of 70 people—their largest so far—showed up, and Hitler's frenzied 30-minute speech was such a success that the party pulled in 300 marks in contributions. There were some hecklers but Hitler, having foreseen that particular possibility, recruited some old army men to deal with them. The troublemakers were thrown down a flight of stairs with their heads split open to emphasize the point. It was a pattern that was to be repeated many times by Hitler's men over the years.

The success of that meeting and those that followed was not produced by force. It was the result of Hitler's genuine magnetism, that personal charisma which began to make itself more evident with every public appearance. He became something of a presence, and his speeches a major attraction, on the Munich political scene. The size of the meetings grew rapidly until finally even people

Hitler electrified audiences with his impassioned and theatrical oratory. His speeches—about the supreme importance of loyalty to the "Fatherland" and the injustice of Germany's defeat, which he blamed on the Jews—were received with wild enthusiasm by demoralized, desperate, inflation-ridden Berliners.

The swastika, symbol of the National Socialist party, had for centuries been given many meanings by people all over the world. To some North American Indians, it represented the cycle of life. After its adoption by Hitler, it soon came to symbolize just one thing: Nazism.

who had little interest in politics came to hear him. For the party, he was invaluable as a spokesman whose scheduled appearances guaranteed an audience. The party was actually able to charge admission to rallies at which he was scheduled to speak. In the year following the triumph of October 1919, Hitler spread the gospel according to the German Workers party at 31 of the 48 meetings they staged.

The style he brought to the platform was both new and original. Unlike the dry, professorial speakers who usually explained the political situation, Hitler presented himself as one of the people, and spoke with spellbinding fervor and sincerity. He could provoke gales of laughter with his mockery of his enemies at one moment, and then create a darker atmosphere with language both bitter and crude. He could arouse pity or terror, pride or indignation.

He practiced his speaking technique quite deliberately, trying different hand gestures before a mirror, but he could never have achieved his success had he not spoken from his own desperate heart. His ability to harmonize with the mood of Germany in the 1920s came from his genuine understanding of the German condition. He could address the humiliation and despair of a defeated, demoralized people because of his own firsthand experience of such emotions. Hitler had the gift of projecting his personal frustration and outrage onto the giant screen of German suffering.

His speeches, although persuasive, made only minor claims on the intelligence. They contained few facts and less logic. They simply swept over the audiences like the majestic tones of Wagner's music, putting reason to sleep but arousing the emotions. "He could play like a virtuoso on the . . . piano of lower-middle-class hearts," wrote an observer years later. Those intellectuals whom he failed to win over began to fear him. They could see in him a primal force hostile to rationality.

And he had another advantage as an orator. He was preaching to the converted, speaking to people who were eager to believe what he said. Postwar

Our motto shall be—If you will not be a German, I will bash your skull in.

—ADOLF HITLER
speaking at a Nazi party meeting in
Munich in 1922

Germany was in bad shape, and, understandably, prone to self-pity. Hitler knew the grievances of his audience because he shared them, and when he spoke he gave the people exactly what they wanted.

He did not have to tell the people what was wrong with their country, and they had no desire to listen to abstract lectures on politics or economics. What Hitler gave them, with burning intensity, was a focus for their resentment—someone to hate and blame for the nation's problems. Germany had not been defeated at the front, he argued, it had been stabbed in the back. The defeat had not been their fault. The *Kaiser* (the German emperor) had betrayed them by abdicating, the Reds had betrayed them by working for international communism, and the Jews had betrayed them by using their economic strength to undermine the German war effort instead of supporting it.

The grievances of Germany were substantial enough, even if Hitler's explanations of them were not. Defeat had brought more than humiliation. It had caused a rate of inflation that grew every month and threatened to wreck the economy. People were selling their household goods and family heirlooms just to stay alive, and a study made in 1919 revealed that more than one-third of all German schoolchildren were undernourished.

All of Germany's problems, economic as well as psychological, had been aggravated by the harsh terms of the Treaty of Versailles, which the Allies had forced Germany to sign at the end of the war. The terms of the treaty were so cruel that even some of the Allies were opposed to it. A number of

[World War I] caused me to think deeply on all things human. Four years of war give a man more than thirty years at a university in the way of education in the problems of life.
—ADOLF HITLER

Hungry Germans wait for free meals in the 1920s. Germany's economy, shaky even before the war, was reeling in its aftermath; staggering inflation and the resulting shortage of food caused widespread starvation and suffering.

Members of the NSDAP— the Nazi party—parade through the streets of Munich in 1923. Following the musicians are uniformed army veterans, recruited by Hitler to give the new organization a military look and to provide the necessary muscle for controlling anti-Nazi hecklers.

The SA man is the sacred freedom fighter. The [Nazi party member] is the instructor and skilled agitator. Political propaganda seeks to enlighten the adversary, to dispute with him, to understand his viewpoint, to go into his ideas, up to a certain point to agree with him—but when the SA appears on the scene, this stops. They are out for all or nothing.
—FRANZ PFEFFER VON SALOMON
senior SA officer

British and American diplomats walked out on the negotiations in protest, and one British official bluntly declared that the only motives of those who approved the treaty were revenge and triumph. The Treaty of Versailles, he prophesied, would prove to have contained "the seeds of future wars."

The terms of this treaty had been made deliberately hard because the Allies simply did not trust Germany. In an attempt to prevent any future resurgence of German power, and to keep the shattered nation so weak that it could never again wage war, the Allies set about depriving Germany of its natural resources and keeping it divided. They forbade Germany to have submarines, military aircraft, or a large standing army. Germany and Austria were not permitted to unite, and, worse yet, Germany was stripped of many of its former territories. Alsace-Lorraine was returned to France, Belgium took over Malmedy, Poland took Posen and parts of Prussia, the Tyrol region went to Italy, and the border area called the Sudetenland was given to Czechoslovakia. Danzig was made a free state. The once great German Empire was reduced to poverty and insignificance.

The Allies then added insult to injury by demanding that Germany pay for all damage to civilian property caused by the war. This is not an unusual term in a peace treaty—the vanquished side usually pays reparations. But Germany was forced to pay so heavily that its economy barely survived the strain. It is estimated that over 38% of

Germany's total capital was exacted for these payments, an average of 1,350 marks per person.

With so fertile a field for action and such devotion to his cause, it is no surprise that Hitler met with success. The six-man debating club called the German Workers party had become a real political force under his guidance, and in 1920 added the words "National Socialist" to demonstrate its increasingly widespread influence. Hitler left the army that same year to devote all his time to the growing National Socialist German Workers party, or, as it was popularly abbreviated, the Nazi party.

In 1920 the Nazi party had 193 members, more than half of them laborers. The meetings often drew thousands, and none passed without some people in the audience succumbing to Hitler's spell and swelling the movement's ranks. Hitler then discovered that, in addition to his skill at speaking, he also had a talent for orchestrating a spectacle. He organized marches and demonstrations, which gave his still small party the appearance of being considerably larger than it really was, and devoted much time and energy to designing dramatic posters, always in flaming red. He borrowed the swastika symbol from an obscure political group that had taken it from ancient East Indian devotional art, and modelled the Nazi salute on the raised arm and outstretched hand technique originally adopted by the Italian fascists in imitation of the ancient Roman legionaries. All these things gave his party a semblance of stature, and people began to take it seriously.

He also succeeded in creating an image of strength for the Nazis by the use of his old army messmates as strong-arm men. This was, he felt, what the people really wanted—strong, brutal leadership—and he had no trouble finding people who were happy to provide it. Ex-soldiers, unable to cope with civilian life, were eager to join the Nazis, who had assumed a paramilitary character by now, and spent as much of their time breaking up communist meetings as they did in conducting their own. In time, the party felt the need for its own organized militia.

Men like Ernst Röhm, a fat, scarred army cap-

Once-proud citizens of Berlin line up at a city soup kitchen. The anger and frustration of the German people after World War I provided the perfect climate for Hitler's fiery speeches, in which he blamed the country's vast problems on everything but the Germans themselves.

[Hitler] talks about race problems. It is impossible to reproduce what he said. It must be experienced. He is a genius. The natural, creative instrument of a fate determined by God. I am deeply moved.... He talks about the state. In the afternoon about winning over the state and political revolution. It sounds like a prophecy. Up in the skies a white cloud takes on the shape of a swastika.
—JOSEPH GOEBBELS

Hermann Göring (1893-1946), the World War I flying ace who became one of the Führer's closest associates, was the kind of man Hitler most admired: a blue-eyed "Nordic" who detested Jews and loved war. Jailed as a war criminal, he killed himself in 1946.

Since I am an immature and wicked man, war and unrest appeal to me more than the good bourgeois order.
—ERNST RÖHM
SA leader

tain who had once been Hitler's commanding officer, lived for violence. They were lost in peacetime. Hitler was glad to put Röhm to use. In 1921—by which time Hitler had effectively ousted Drexler and taken over the party—Röhm helped organize a sort of private army for the Nazis. The *Sturmabteilung* (Storm Division) had their own uniform, from which they took their nickname—the Brownshirts. Röhm's army connections enabled them to operate with impunity, and they soon became one of the most prominent and potent of the many organizations in postwar Munich which were fighting for political power against the bleak backdrop of social disintegration.

Other army officers rapidly followed suit as the reputation of the Nazi party grew. In November 1922 a dashing young war hero named Hermann Göring—a former squadron commander in the now defunct imperial air force and a holder of Germany's highest medal—heard Hitler speak and was held spellbound. To Göring, a restless, discontented veteran looking for a cause worthy of his devotion, the Nazi party seemed, so to speak, made to order. His own natural flamboyance, combined with a love of drama and dressing up, made the splashy and ostentatious Nazis a particularly attractive proposition. He sympathized completely with the views of the party leadership—resentment of the Treaty of Versailles, grandiose notions of Germany's glory, and hatred of Jews and Reds. Moreover, there was nothing he loved as much as a good fight. Hitler saw his value at once, and Göring soon became the supreme commander of the SA, the Stormtroopers.

Another ex-officer who joined early on was Rudolf Hess, a middle-class rightist who also desperately needed something to cling to following the war. Although he came from a family of merchants, he had no head for either business or study. What he did have was a great capacity for devotion. He wandered from one form of occultism to another—astrology one day, faith healing the next—and when he heard the electrifying voice of Hitler in 1921 he became his slave at once. Known in the party as "the brown mouse," Hess became Hitler's secretary and most loyal shadow.

Any Weimar liberal confronted with an array of lieutenants such as the one Hitler had gathered about himself would undoubtedly have realized that the civilized approach to politics in Germany was about to take a fatal beating. Röhm had a reputation for sexual perversion. Göring had a narcotics problem and enjoyed killing for its own sake. Hess was both bigoted and confused. Of such stuff was Hitler's staff made, and he knew it. He saw very clearly that misfits like these could be molded into the kind of fighting force essential to the so-called holy mission he had mapped out for himself and his party.

Buoyed by his early successes, the increasingly confident Hitler now aspired to a more substantial goal than mere leadership of an extremist political organization in a provincial city like Munich. His dreams were for his party, his nation, and his people. He was accused, when he wrested the party leadership from Drexler in 1921, of "a lust for power and personal ambition," but in fact, Hitler was really quite selfless in his aspirations. He was truly fused with his party, which he saw as the only instrument for the salvation of Germany.

But it was not simply as a political party that Hitler saw the Nazis succeeding. It was as a legion, an army. He had neither faith nor interest in gradual parliamentary reforms. He wanted action. He believed that the country would only realize its destiny when all Germans everywhere united to smash the feeble Weimar government, abolish the hateful Treaty of Versailles, sweep out the Jews and other aliens, and restore Germany to her rightful power and glory.

The Nazi party, with its increasing numbers of former soldiers eager for action, was fast becoming more militarized than ever. Gradually, and ominously, it came to resemble nothing so much as an extension of Hitler's will. Confident that he truly represented the German people, that his will was that of Germany, Hitler forged ahead steadily as he looked to the next stage of his program for national deliverance—a *putsch*, a violent uprising.

Ernst Röhm (1887-1934) (at left) and Rudolf Hess (1894-   ) were among Hitler's most trusted lieutenants. Röhm, who created Hitler's private army, the infamous Brownshirts, was killed on Hitler's orders in 1934. Hess flew to England on an unauthorized diplomatic mission in 1941. Imprisoned by the British, he was sentenced to life imprisonment at the end of World War II, and remains under Soviet custody in East Berlin's Spandau prison to this day.

5
The Revolutionary

By 1923 Hitler's reputation as a mere agitator had been largely superseded. He had actually managed to gain a measure of what passed for political respectability and power in postwar Munich. Bavaria was in conflict with the national government in Berlin, and the Nazi party was taking full advantage of the unrest. Some Bavarians wanted their province to become an independent state, or perhaps to form an alliance with Austria. Almost everyone wanted to see the weak liberal administration in Berlin overthrown and replaced with a strong national government—one capable of rebuilding the army and defying the Treaty of Versailles.

Germany's situation went from bad to worse. Inflation became unendurable. The German mark, worth about four cents in January of 1919, fell to less than 1/70 of a cent by January of 1921, and in that year the Allies demanded of Germany $33 billion in reparations. The repeated and uncaring Allied demands sounded the death knell for what little confidence the defeated Germans still possessed. The currency collapsed and took German industry with it.

The list of German grievances grew even longer when, in 1921, the League of Nations voted to give a large slice of former German territory in Silesia to Poland. In January of 1923 the French, in retaliation for a late payment of reparations, occupied

A Berlin housewife proves she has "money to burn"—literally. By 1923 the value of the German mark had fallen so drastically that it was actually more useful for starting fires than for buying kindling.

Hitler's riveting speaking style attracted more and more followers as Germany's economic crisis worsened. He never undervalued his power to mesmerize crowds with his speeches, which he once called "the burning brand of the word hurled among the masses."

the rich industrial area of the Ruhr Valley. By July of that same year, the mark was worth 1/40,000 of a cent. The country was now completely bankrupt. Deprived of those areas that had contained the bulk of its heavy industry and natural resources, Germany seemed to have no prospect of recovery.

The populace was at its wit's end. Something had to be done, someone had to take control and lead the country back to prosperity. Naturally, Hitler thought that he and his party were the only people capable of doing just that.

The eccentric man who sometimes called himself the "King of Munich" had not yet come to dominate the city's politics completely. Indeed, his humble and unimpressive personal life lacked the kind of style normally cultivated by men who aspire to positions of influence. Like many other members of his party, he lived from day to day with no very certain income. In fact, he seemed quite indifferent to money. He occupied a tiny, unheated furnished room in a poor section of town and owned almost nothing. His wardrobe consisted of an old, ill-fitting blue suit and a cheap raincoat, and he seldom had his hair cut. There is no evidence that he had anything resembling a social life, or that he ever took any interest in women.

Hitler may have lacked the trappings of power, but the Weimar government knew he would have to be included in their political equations. The fact remains, however, that few officials took Hitler and his Stormtroopers very seriously. Although in 1922 he had spent a month in jail for leading a Nazi assault on a rival political meeting, he still seemed more of a nuisance than a real threat. Some officials suggested that he be deported back to Austria (he was still registered as an Austrian citizen), but others suspected that the powerful combination of his magnetic personality and the increasingly formidable militia he controlled might prove useful in the inevitable confrontation to come.

The government officials were also quite sure that a man so lacking in conventional political experience would be easy enough to control should the situation ever appear to be getting out of hand.

Benito Mussolini (1883-1945), the fascist dictator who ruled Italy from 1922 to 1945, resembled Hitler in many ways. Like the Nazi leader, he was a war veteran from the middle class, a passionate anti-communist and nationalist, and he was determined to rule his country by force. Mussolini and Hitler became allies in 1936.

This drastic misreading of both Adolf Hitler and the mood of the German people by experienced and supposedly discerning politicians must stand as one of the costliest miscalculations in history.

Hitler and his party received substantial support from such important industrialists as United Steel Works chairman Fritz von Thyssen, who gave the Nazi party $25,000 in 1923. Others backed the party more modestly and discreetly, and the overall contributions were quite sufficient to keep the Nazis going. General Erich Ludendorff, the venerable commander-in-chief of the German army during the war and an ardent nationalist, lent his impressive name to Hitler's cause, although he was openly unenthusiastic about Hitler himself.

In his continuing search for ways in which to enhance the dramatic public image of the Nazi party, Hitler had already borrowed several ideas from the Italian fascist leader Benito Mussolini. In October 1922 Mussolini had threatened that he and his black-shirted supporters would march on Rome and seize control of the government. Faced with a situation that could easily have deteriorated into civil war, the king and his senior ministers gave in to Mussolini's demands and made him premier. With his "Blackshirts" strutting through the streets of Rome, Mussolini had become the undisputed ruler of the country without a single vote having been cast.

Hitler felt that this subversion of democracy in

Hitler, in the center of a group of aides, receives a salute from parading Nazi troops. The Weimar government fatally misjudged the threat posed by Hitler's increasingly powerful party.

Italy constituted solid evidence of the correctness of his own perception of politics. A mass movement under strong leadership could successfully bypass the parliamentary process. Accordingly, Hitler regimented his Stormtroopers in much the same way that Mussolini had organized his Blackshirts. The Nazi "goosestep" was inspired by the high-stepping march of Mussolini's cohorts.

Now the time seemed ripe to follow Mussolini's example yet again. Inspired by the Italian dictator's successful seizure of power in Rome, Hitler decided it was time to act. He began organizing a putsch, an uprising that would take control of Bavaria as a prelude to overthrowing the government in Berlin.

The Germans were weak, Hitler argued, because they were not unified. If all Germans joined together in a Greater German *Reich*—a single German nation including Germany, Austria, and all other German-speaking areas—they could regain that power that was theirs by right of their heroic past. The Master Race could throw off the chains of the humiliating and repressive Treaty of Versailles and take its rightful place as ruler of Europe. Any German who failed to join such a great cause, he said, deserved to be crushed. Power and freedom could be achieved only by force.

On November 7, 1923, Hitler and his colleagues, who had intended to stage the putsch on November 11, heard that a large patriotic demonstration had been planned in Munich. Since the three top men in the Bavarian government were to be there, it seemed to the Nazis an ideal opportunity to make their move, despite the risks involved in bringing their schedule forward at short notice. It was the most critical political decision Hitler had made so far, and he was, not unnaturally, extremely nervous. He even went so far as to drink a couple of glasses of beer for courage—a thing he rarely did. He felt sure that failure would mean death, but there was no turning back now.

For an affair in which the issues at stake were so serious, the putsch soon degenerated into near comic confusion. No one was sure what was happening or who was on whose side. Messages failed

Munich's **Bürgerbräukeller** was the scene of Hitler's *putsch* in 1923. Although the botched Nazi effort had some slightly comical aspects, its long-term consequences were deadly serious. Hitler's subsequent trial made him a local celebrity, and his imprisonment enabled him to write his book, *Mein Kampf.*

to reach their destination, key figures lost their nerve, and decisions were made and changed every minute. Like most political events in Munich, the meeting was held in a beer hall, and the crowd was half drunk when the time came for the official commencement of the revolution.

Hitler jumped onto a table and fired a shot into the ceiling. In the stunned silence that followed, he announced in a high, excited voice that the uprising had begun and that the government of Bavaria and the national government in Berlin had been overthrown. Ludendorff was now in command of the army, he said, and he, Adolf Hitler, was head of the new government. He ordered the three Bavarian ministers of state into a back room and threatened to shoot them unless they declared their support for the putsch. Seeing the fanatical glint in his eyes as he waved his pistol at them, they quickly agreed to Hitler's demands.

Meanwhile, Göring had surrounded the hall with Brownshirts, and other SA troops under Röhm had occupied key positions throughout the city. It appeared that Hitler's bluff had worked.

The next morning Hitler, Göring, Ludendorff, and other leaders of the Nazi party marched together to take over the government offices, convinced that the people were solidly behind them and that the revolution had succeeded.

It soon became apparent, however, that the Beer Hall Putsch had already failed. The three govern-

Hitler's treason trial, following the aborted "Beer Hall Putsch" of 1923, made a mockery of the Weimar judicial system. The judge allowed Hitler to make speeches and to ridicule government officials. One German newspaperman said the proceedings quite resembled a "carnival."

After the putsch, Hitler spent 13 pleasant months in Landsberg prison. He passed several hours a day greeting crowds of admiring visitors, many of whom brought flowers and food. One observer reported that Hitler's cell (actually a fairly comfortable room) "looked like a delicatessen."

ment ministers who had publicly agreed to support the uprising had been allowed to leave the building and had immediately withdrawn their statements. Due to the fact that Röhm's SA contingent had taken over every office in the regional military headquarters building except the communications center, army officers loyal to the government had been able to call in troops from several outlying districts.

The intended beneficiaries of Hitler's revolution, the general public, had not the slightest idea what was going on. For a while Nazis were arresting policemen for obstructing their march and policemen were arresting Nazis for marching. It has never been quite clear who double-crossed whom, but when the Nazis approached the government offices, they were met by armed police.

Hitler and Ludendorff soon discovered that they had made a fatal mistake in imagining that Germans would never shoot other Germans, especially Germans leading a popular revolution. Sixteen Nazis were killed and many more wounded. Göring, although badly hurt by a bullet, managed to get away. Hitler, evidently while ducking, fell and severely dislocated his shoulder. General Ludendorff was arrested.

In the confusion, Hitler made his escape, only to be apprehended the next day at the home of a friend. Clad in nothing but a bathrobe, to which he had pinned one of his wartime medals, he was thrown into jail and informed that he would stand trial for treason.

Demonstrating yet again his ingrained talent for survival, Hitler managed to turn an apparent disaster into a major opportunity. The trial, which ran through February and March of 1924, offered him a better propaganda platform than some of his most memorable rallies ever had. Hitler spoke eloquently in his own defense, arguing that he had acted for his beloved country and that his "mission in life was to lead Germany back to its proper position in the world." He turned his defense into another attack on the "criminals" of the Weimar government who had "stabbed Germany in the back and were still holding it down."

The court was, on the whole, sympathetic, and so was the audience. Ludendorff, who behaved with all the arrogance typical of many German officers of general rank, made the judge shake in his robes, much to the surprise of the foreign journalists present. To many outside observers the proceedings appeared to be a travesty of a trial. The fact that Hitler was allowed to rant at his prosecutors for hours on end constituted a mockery of accepted legal procedure. The judge excused himself from responsibility for this farcical situation, claiming that it was simply impossible to keep Hitler from talking. With constant Nazi cheering resounding throughout the courtroom the prosecution shrank from pressing its case too hard.

On April 1, 1924, Hitler received the minimum sentence of five years, almost with the apologies of the court, and was recommended for early parole. Flowers and gifts poured in for him. He had become something of a hero in Munich.

The trial proved, according to the *Times* of London, "that a plot against the constitution of the *Reich* is not considered a serious crime in Bavaria."

In fact, Hitler served only nine months of his sentence, confined in the Landsberg Fortress, which was more like a hotel than a prison. He had a large, sunny private room that was about twice the size of the dreary little apartment he had rented in Munich, and better heated. He received regular and decent meals. The prison authorities allowed him books and the congenial company of his fellow inmates, all Nazis who had been involved with him in the putsch. The whole interlude was like a vacation for Hitler. The sudden improvement in his diet caused him to gain a little weight, and he used this period of enforced leisure to make plans for the future.

He had learned a major lesson from his effort in Munich: Germans would never support a violent overthrow of the government. However they might cheer his speeches, they believed in law and order. He would have to bring on a national revolution by legal, peaceful means.

To clarify his ideas and continue his propaganda,

General Erich Ludendorff (1865 - 1937) was, like Hitler, arrested after the 1923 putsch. An imperious hero of World War I, he intimidated the judge at his trial by acting more like a military prosecutor than a defendant accused of treason. He was acquitted and later became a pacifist.

Playwright Bertolt Brecht (1898-1956) was one of the leftist intellectual artists despised by Hitler and his followers. Many talented German writers, painters, architects, musicians, dramatists, and movie directors abandoned, or were expelled from, their homeland when the Nazis came to power early in 1933.

he set about writing a book. He dictated *Mein Kampf* ("My Struggle") to various members of the faithful following that had accompanied him into Landsberg. The ever-adoring Rudolf Hess, who had a little college education to his credit and could at least spell, was chosen as chief scribe, and he slavishly took down the bulk of Hitler's self-justifying autobiography.

Mein Kampf is an extraordinary work. Although Hitler intended it as a social and economic treatise, it is really nothing more than a political tract directed against communists and Jews. The Reds, Hitler explains, had caused the inflation that was ruining Germany, and the Jews had conspired against the country for their own financial gain. The Jews, Hitler declared, were the evil force behind all the troubles of Europe.

There was nothing new in all this. Such prejudices had been popular throughout Europe for years, and the Germans in particular had cultivated them recently because the situation was so much worse in Germany than elsewhere. *Mein Kampf* made the stab-in-the-back theory believable to people who wanted to believe it anyway.

Sensational and self-congratulatory as the arguments are, the book is almost unreadable and far from convincing. The few ideas contained in the work (which Hitler thought a masterpiece) tend to get lost in the long and rambling sentences. Despite this, there remains something horribly fascinating about the unashamed cynicism with which Hitler viewed power and people.

He calls for an alliance of Germany with Italy and Great Britain, and the establishment of a military superstate strong enough to withstand any aggression by the Soviet Union. He calmly recommends brute force as a government policy. "The one means that wins the easiest victory over reason," he states, "is terror and force." Such words as *smash, force, ruthless, terror,* and *hatred* appear repeatedly. In fact, *Mein Kampf* reads like a transcript of one of Hitler's public speeches: for all its obscure language and involved grammar, the overtones of the politics of hysteria pervade the entire work. Hitler remained a potent rabble-rouser behind bars, his passionate anti-Semitism as forceful in print as it was on the speaker's platform.

At some points, *Mein Kampf* seems to be a manual for dictators. Hitler offers such candid advice as: "When you tell a lie, tell a big one." Hitler's opinion of the German mind is stated clearly throughout. "The receptive powers of the masses are very restricted," he writes, "and their understanding is feeble." It is perhaps surprising that a book so insulting to its readers was so popular. Nevertheless, it sold over 300,000 copies in Germany before Hitler came to power, and the royalties supported its author for years.

While most of the rest of the world dismissed *Mein Kampf* as absurd, a few people were sufficiently shrewd to recognize it for what it was—a serious blueprint for world conquest.

Residents of Berlin's Jewish ghetto. Hitler's book *Mein Kampf,* which blamed the Jews for most of Germany's economic woes, provoked bands of bloodthirsty anti-Semites into extensive acts of violence and terror against Jews.

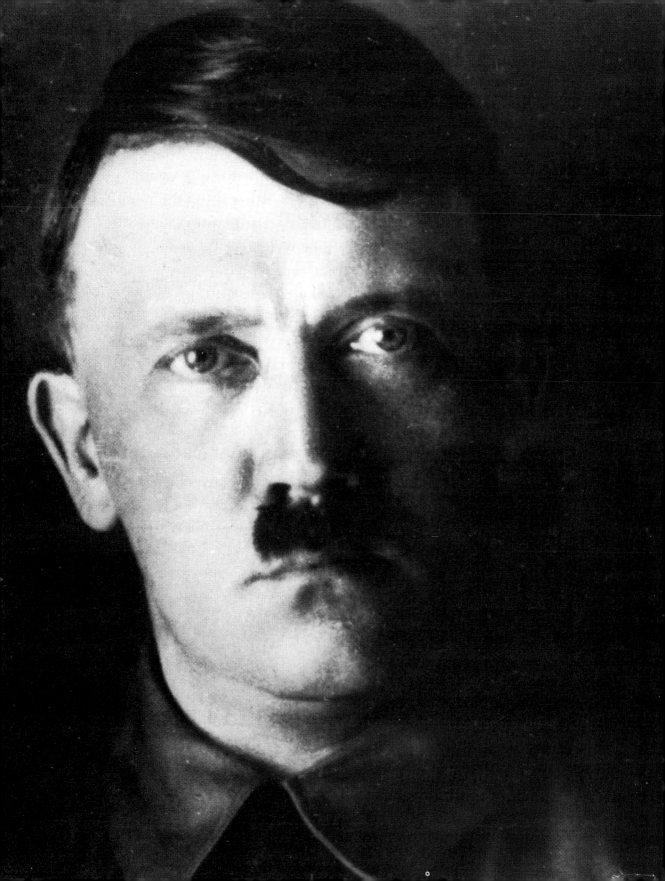

6

The Chancellor

Hitler left prison in December 1924, more fit and stronger than when he had entered. He remained utterly determined to promote his ideas, even though the authorities had forbidden him to speak in public. Worse yet, the Nazi party, now banned, had deteriorated badly in Hitler's absence. Lack of strong leadership had caused it to split into rival factions, and the country no longer responded to the party's message with much enthusiasm. Slowly but surely, Germany had become a somewhat calmer country, and the Nazis found themselves deprived of the environment of acute social chaos in which their particular brand of politics had traditionally flourished.

Bowing to American pressure, the French government had instituted a more reasonable schedule for reparation payments. Further aided by the introduction of a new and more stable currency the German economy had begun to revive.

While the survival of the liberal Weimar government was by no means assured, it did represent a remarkable departure from the highly nationalistic and militaristic political system which had preceded it. Reflecting these tensions between past and present, Germany became an intellectual battlefield during the 1920s. The freedom of expression guaranteed by the new constitution caused a

Wall Street traders eagerly check tickertape to confirm rising stock prices. The mid-1920s improvement in the German economy was good news for the country, but bad news for Hitler's National Socialist (Nazi) party, which tended to attract more followers when times were tough.

Once released from prison, Adolf Hitler consistently claimed that the experience had much improved his life. It was while in jail, he said, "that I acquired that fearless faith, that optimism, that confidence in our destiny, which nothing could shake thereafter."

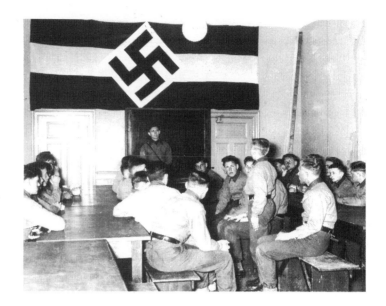

Young Germans face a large swastika as they listen to a Nazi youth-camp leader talk about National Socialist values. Boys aged 10 to 14 were organized in the *Jungvolk* (Young Folk); at 15 they entered the *Hitler Jugend* (Hitler Youth), where they received daggers engraved with the motto "Blood and Honor" and became entitled to wear the official Nazi uniform—a brown shirt.

flowering of culture quite unlike anything previously seen in that country.

The Weimar Republic came to represent not just a major experiment in progressive government but also a haven for artistic modernism. Germany began to breed the kind of artists Hitler loved to hate, and Berlin became the city to which most of them flocked. The future dictator continued to dream of the music and architecture of the 1890s. Thousands of romantically inclined ex-servicemen like him consoled themselves with the works of such nationalist writers as Ernst Jünger, who longed to see the nation made into a superstate run like a Prussian barracks, and whose writings called for "a new race, cunning, strong, and purposeful," and insisted that "new forms must be molded with blood, and power must be seized with a hard fist."

While these diehard conservatives licked their wounds and waited for their main chance, the other Germany supported revolution in the fields of music, opera, theater, design, literature, the fine arts, and film.

With *Drums in the Night*, first performed in 1922, playwright Bertolt Brecht introduced to the world a completely new kind of drama, one that reflected his commitment to communism, his fascination with violence, and his hatred of middle-class manners and morals. In 1928 alone his revolutionary musical drama *The Threepenny Opera*, with music by Kurt Weill, received a total of 4,000 performances in Europe.

Other playwrights proceeded to earn the hatred of rightists by devising more sophisticated, but no less passionate, examinations of "polite" society. Men like Arthur Schnitzler and Georg Kaiser ridiculed the respectable, while leaving it to Brecht to terrify the middle classes with visions of workers and criminals wreaking vengeance on their self-styled superiors.

The Berlin policeman who sat through a progressive play and then suggested that "the whole trend ought to be liquidated" typified the backward-looking

Campaign posters of 1932, when Hitler tried to unseat President Paul von Hindenburg (1847-1934). Hitler lost the election, but he soon forced Hindenburg to appoint him chancellor, thus becoming Germany's most powerful politician.

Eva Braun (1912-1945), Hitler's devoted companion for 16 years, gave up hope of becoming his wife. "I can never think of marrying Eva," he said in 1934. He changed his mind the day before their deaths.

Germans who felt threatened by modern art and its politics. They found the prospect of thinking for themselves utterly frightening and would soon fall into step behind men like Adolf Hitler, the demagogue who seemed only too happy to do their thinking for them. Lacking the courage to shoulder the blame for the past, they would also refuse to take responsibility for the future.

Berlin also became a major center of the movie industry. Films like Fritz Lang's *Metropolis*, Joseph von Sternberg's *The Blue Angel*, and Billy Wilder's *Emil and the Detectives* set standards in that medium which have rarely been surpassed. They bravely invited people to examine the dark side of human nature, and suggested that a failure to deal with it might lead to disaster—which, of course, it eventually did.

Composers like Alban Berg and architects like Walter Gropius were raising the status of their respective arts to new heights. The genius displayed by Berg in his disturbing and unusual opera *Wozzeck*, first performed in Berlin in 1925, was brilliantly matched by the creative generosity of the man who conducted the premiere. Erich Kleiber paid tribute to *Wozzeck*'s merits by authorizing an unprecedented 130 rehearsals prior to the opening night. Under the inventive leadership of Walter Gropius, artists at the Bauhaus, Weimar's "shrine" to modernism, struggled to realize the revolutionary concept of *Gesamtkunstwerk* (total work of art). They combined painting, sculpture, architecture, and textile and furniture design.

All these advances in art were the natural result of creativity at work in a free society. Indeed, at its best the Weimar Republic constituted a blueprint for an ideal democratic society and system of government. Germany, however, was not yet ready for such departures from previous experience—and the future dictator knew it.

Undeterred by these transformations, Hitler simply disregarded what he saw as the decadent liberalism and "cultural bolshevism" temporarily afflicting his homeland. He set about rebuilding his party and selling himself and his political ideas to both big business, which had always favored his anti-union policies, and, more importantly, to the middle classes, who were still smarting from their loss of both status and savings to the ravages of hyper-inflation. Gradually his relentless efforts began to show results.

The Nazi leaders in northern Germany began to come under his influence. By 1926, though still subject to a court order which barred him from speaking in public, he had again made himself and his party a force to be reckoned with. All he and his organization needed was the right opportunity.

The effects of the United States stock market crash of November 1929 were felt around the world. The depression hit Germany as hard as it did America. Yet again, paper money became almost worthless. The story was told in Berlin of a woman on her way to market with a big basket of money. She was carrying so much currency that she had to set it down to rest, and a thief came up, dumped the money in the street, and ran off—with the basket!

The suffering of the German people once again provided a perfect setting for increased Nazi agitation. This time Hitler had learned his lesson and worked through legal, electoral channels. By now he was permitted to speak again, and once more he worked himself and his audiences into a frenzy with his hateful, irrational messages. Hitler appealed to the deepest emotions of his hearers, and there are descriptions of men groaning and women sobbing in his audiences.

As the country became more desperate and the party more unified, the Nazis' strength at the polls increased. In 1930 they attracted 6 million votes and came in second among the many parties competing for power. Though growing more influential by the day, Hitler consistently refused the many offers he received from other political parties. Even the prospect of a cabinet post in exchange for Nazi support failed to move him. Hitler and his party did not intend to share the supremacy for which they believed they were destined. In 1932 he ran for president against Paul von Hindenburg.

An aristocratic old general and war hero, Hindenburg looked like a movie stereotype of a German officer, with his side whiskers, his cape, and his spiked helmet. At age 85, having served as a figurehead president from 1925 to 1932, all he really wanted to do was retire. But his friends persuaded the old man to run for one more term. He narrowly defeated Hitler, who gained 36.8% of the vote.

The depression worsened, and violence in the streets became common. In 1932 there were 6 million unemployed in Germany. Predictably, the Nazis rose to the occasion in their own tried and tested way, and every party meeting prompted demonstrations and riots. The SA fought the police and the communists, and some members of the government demanded that the organization be banned. Others, however, were afraid that such a move might trigger further violence, and many felt that the Nazi militia might best be used to preserve order in the event of a Red uprising. Unlike the pro-Soviet communists, the Stormtroopers were still considered to be on Germany's side, despite their tendency to view brute force as a legitimate political tool.

The president of Germany had responsibility for the appointment of a chancellor, the man who would actually run the government. That was the job Hitler wanted—the only job he would take—but Hindenburg would have nothing to do with him. As late as January 26, 1933, the old man would still insist to his closest colleagues that he did not intend to "make that Austrian private first class chancellor." Hindenburg wanted someone safe and civilized, someone of his own class. On May 31, 1932, Franz von Papen became chancellor of Germany.

Papen was a rich and elegant aristocrat, an expert jockey in his spare time, and a great socialite. "Smooth, silly, and a survivor," as historian Norman Stone described him, Papen rarely suffered serious setbacks, mainly because he never took chances. "I need a hat, not a head," Hindenburg's advisor bluntly explained.

Adolf Hitler, however, the man who believed he

had more of a head for the job than Papen, wasted no time in making it clear that his support for the new government was only provisional. Not for a single moment did he doubt that he would be chancellor one day. Accordingly, he ordered the party rank and file to resume the activities that had become their hallmark. During the summer of 1932 Nazis and communists fought it out and died on the streets of every major city in Germany.

Hitler's personal life during this period disappears almost completely behind the events of his public career. "The Party is Hitler and Hitler is the Party," Hess once observed. Hitler had never had a long-term relationship with a woman, and there was much conjecture about whether he was even capable of such a liaison.

The closest he ever came to a romance during his rise to power was when he developed an odd, mysterious affection for his niece, Geli Raubal, daughter of his half-sister Angela, and 19 years his

The German people is not marked by original sin, but by original nobility. The place of Christian love has been taken by the National Socialist, Germanic idea of comradeship ... which has already been symbolically expressed through the replacement of the rosary by the spade of labor.
—ALFRED ROSENBERG
leading Nazi ideologist

Young female athletes parade behind a row of Nazi flags at a Munich sports festival in 1933. The Nazis encouraged women to excel in sports, but not in politics or business. Women were considered important only as wives and mothers.

junior. Rumors of an association between Hitler and Geli first began to circulate when she and her family moved into his building in Munich to keep house for him. Speculation as to the nature of their relationship vastly increased when she shot herself with her uncle's pistol in 1931. Some said that she had been in love with him and died of frustration at his indifference. Others said that she had been in love with someone else and he had opposed it. Still others insisted that he had been in love with her and had frightened her into suicide. Probably we will never know the truth of this curious incident.

After a decent period of mourning, Hitler renewed his acquaintance with a young woman whom he had first met in 1929—Eva Braun, a bland, plump shop clerk with blond hair and a pleasant, flirtatious manner. Eva, 23 years younger than Hitler, described him to her sister as "the elderly gentleman," and the evidence suggests that their relationship was not physical. He occasionally sent her flowers, and certainly seemed to enjoy her company. That, however, was as far as it went. There can be no doubt that, in his own perverse and disturbing way, Adolf Hitler was an extremely passionate man. And yet the only real love affair he ever had was with himself, and the country he hoped to remake in his own image.

Whatever his successes or failures on the domestic front, Hitler was making steady progress in his political career, and it is hardly surprising that he was totally preoccupied with it. In the five years since their disastrous performance in the elections of 1928, when they had attracted 100,000 fewer votes than in 1926, the Nazis had become dominant throughout Germany. Hitler had finally achieved the political prominence essential to a successful bid for power.

Papen wanted his support. Indeed, the government needed the backing of Hitler and his followers. But when Papen offered him the vice-chancellorship, Hitler refused it. By this time he understood his opponents much better than they understood him. He had learned a great deal about political negotiation, and he wanted supreme power or none at all. When Papen refused to step down in return for Hitler's votes in support of the coalition Papen had proposed, the full power of the Nazi press was turned against him and his "cabinet of barons." Mocked in the newspapers, attacked in the government by Hitler's supporters, Papen was finally forced to bow out.

Finally, when Hitler then refused to endorse Papen's successor, Kurt von Schleicher, the government was forced to its knees. Papen returned to Hitler and humbly asked the Nazi leader what it would take to gain his party's support for the Schleicher administration. Hitler's moment had come. He seized his opportunity and demanded Schleicher's job—the chancellorship, with full powers. Realizing that the strength of Hitler's party and the extent of his popularity with the German people could no longer be ignored, the aristocrats swallowed their pride and agreed.

Hindenburg, now almost senile and utterly incapable of fully appreciating what was going on, proceeded to rubber-stamp Papen's recommendations. On January 30, 1933, four days after he had promised never to turn over the office of chancellor to Hitler, he went back on his word.

On the condition that Papen remain as vice-chancellor—a token concession that changed nothing—the old warrior, "the last symbol of Prussia's greatness and of its decline," appointed the "Austrian private first class," Adolf Hitler, chief executive of the Republic of Germany.

The country boy from Austria, the outsider, the starving artist and friendless soldier, had beaten, bullied, schemed, and shouted his way to the top. His dream of power was fulfilled at last. To many politicians such success might seem the crowning achievement of a life's work. For Hitler, for Germany, and the world beyond its borders, January 30, 1933, would prove one of the most decisive dates in history. Every excess committed by Hitler and his party up to that time would turn out to have been but a pale reflection of the furious future at the heart of his fanatical vision.

Reich Chancellor Adolf Hitler greets President Paul von Hindenburg in Berlin in February 1934. Hindenburg had fought against appointing Hitler chancellor, and was appalled by Hitler's bloody purge of the Brownshirt leadership on June 30, 1934. When he died on August 2, 1934, Chancellor Hitler immediately assumed the presidency.

7

The Führer

Hitler became chancellor of Germany the same year Franklin D. Roosevelt took office as president of the United States, and both faced many similar problems. Both men came to power at the lowest point of an unprecedented economic slump. Unemployment in Germany in 1933 stood at a crippling 25%, and conditions in the United States were little better. In both countries the hardest-hit members of a desperate and helpless populace stood on line at soup kitchens, cursing a situation for which it seemed their governments could find neither explanation nor cure. The two lands were also frantic for reform.

Under the terms of their national constitutions, the options available to both men were severely limited. It was Hitler, however, who almost immediately demonstrated his basic indifference to such constraints.

Hitler considered himself the archetype of a new breed of German politician. He knew that, to achieve his political objectives, he would have to come to an arrangement with the nation's armed forces, the *Reichswehr*. The military, however, was still in the hands of the conservative, old-school officers who had commanded the nation's armies for generations.

Most German officers (and especially those of

A young military enthusiast, wearing a Nazi uniform and swastika-decorated helmet, salutes a member of the newly constituted *Wehrmacht* (Armed Forces) in Berlin in 1935. The Nazis recognized the importance of youth support, and began indoctrinating children at an early age.

A huge portrait of Adolf Hitler, posed behind a plow, dwarfs the speaker at a 1934 agricultural show in Berlin. As Hitler became more firmly entrenched, heroic statues and pictures of him were ostentatiously displayed throughout Germany.

Testifying to Hitler's enormous popularity, cheering farmers crowd around the Nazi leader's car in the Bavarian resort town of Berchtesgaden in 1934. Hitler often visited Berchtesgaden, where he would don *lederhosen* (leather shorts) and take strenuous walks in the mountains.

general rank) took a dim view of politicians. This attitude, a relic of the imperial period, had become even more prevalent during the Weimar era. The top military men, while claiming to be utterly unconcerned with politics, had made no secret of their hostility to the liberal and largely pacifist Weimar government. In the aftermath of World War I, General Hans von Seeckt had encouraged the officer corps to transfer its loyalty to the military leadership since its traditional figurehead, the Kaiser, had fled the country. Seeckt's problems became less pressing following Hindenburg's appointment to the presidency in 1925, since the elderly general commanded much respect among the military.

Now, inspite of the forbidding old Prussian, a new relationship had to be established between the government and the army. Hitler began to make the necessary overtures. In February 1933, within days of his appointment as chancellor, he had made a speech to the high command. On that occasion Hitler was not preaching to the converted. Many of the older and most senior officers present had long looked upon the Nazis with great distaste. Hitler later asserted that it was one of the most unrewarding addresses he had ever made and claimed that the experience had been like "speaking to a wall."

On that day, however—February 3, 1933—Hitler

did manage to lay the foundations of precisely the kind of relationship he wanted with the military. He promised them rearmament and "the steeling of youth and the strengthening of the will to defense by all possible means." He also insisted that "the struggle inside the country [was] not [the army's affair] but the affair of the Nazi organizations." This latter expression was perhaps the most fateful element of the entire lecture. In return for his guarantee of rearmament he had asked the army to turn a blind eye to everything that happened beyond the barracks gate. His recommendations met with the complete approval of two men who were ideally placed to secure their incorporation into army policy—Werner von Blomberg, the Reichswehr minister, and Walther von Reichenau, his chief advisor.

Serving their own interests with a lack of moral scruple more appropriate to Brownshirts than to officers and gentlemen, they successfully sold a new form of domestic neutrality to the army. Shortly after Hitler's speech, in an address to a gathering of senior officers, Reichenau said, "We must recognize that we are in the midst of a revolution. What is rotten in the state must fall and it can only be brought down by terror. The [Nazi] party will proceed ruthlessly against Marxism. The Army's task is to order arms. No succor if any of the persecuted seek refuge with the troops."

In his book *The Face of the Third Reich* German historian Joachim C. Fest gives what is perhaps the best assessment made to date of the course upon which the German army found itself launched at that point when he writes: "It was the old formula . . . of the 'unpolitical soldier' that was now employed more intensively than ever before as an ideological mask for a fundamental fear of decision making. . . . Under the Weimar Republic this attitude had led the army to withdraw its loyalty from the state, whereas now, under the growing power of Hitler, it was to the victims of the state that aid was refused. In other words, where before the Army had refused to say yes, now it refused to say no."

Slowly but surely, over the next five years, the German army (which was renamed the *Wehrmacht*,

> *What is the dog making of our beautiful Germany!*
> —LUDWIG BECK
> German general, speaking in 1937 with reference to Hitler

Gestapo chief Heinrich Himmler (1900-1945) was a man of unswerving loyalty and awesome cruelty. "Whether [non-Germans] perish of hunger," he said in 1943, "interests me only insofar as we need them as slaves for our culture." He was captured by the British military and committed suicide in 1945.

or Armed Forces, in 1935) would become a thoroughly submissive instrument of Nazi policy. In 1938 the unscrupulous Blomberg would be dismissed from office on trumped-up charges of sexual misconduct and replaced by one of the weakest men ever to have donned the uniform of a Wehrmacht general. Walther von Brauchitsch, who described himself as "ready for anything," was a Hitler yes-man to the core. The one thing he emphasized over and over again to his supreme commander, Adolf Hitler, was that he would bring the army closer than ever to National Socialism.

The German army was to become just the kind of fighting force Hitler wanted. In retrospect it seems inevitable that an army capable of turning a blind eye to Nazi excesses would, in time, learn to tolerate all excesses—even its own. Ultimately, the German military would follow orders until it had dispensed with all the normal rules of civilized conduct relating to warfare.

Early in 1934 Hitler decided to face a problem that had finally assumed critical proportions. The SA had become too independent and was causing trouble within the party. Röhm, one of the founders of the Nazis' private militia, had been recalled from Bolivia (where he had been working as a military advisor) in 1931 to resume command of the organization. By the end of 1933, SA membership had reached 4 million and Hitler, who was understandably nervous about the situation, had already begun to shift his support to another, smaller group, the *Schutzstaffel* (Guard Detachment). Organized in 1928 as an élite private bodyguard for Hitler, the SS, as they were called, had their own uniforms, from which they gained their sinister nickname, the Blackshirts. Their symbol was a skull.

The commander of the SS was one of Hitler's earliest and most loyal supporters, Heinrich Himmler. A former army clerk who was working in the office of a fertilizer factory when he joined the party in 1919, Himmler had marched in the 1923 putsch but had not been important enough to arrest.

Now, at age 33, Himmler received his second major appointment when Göring made him head

The Brown House, Nazi party headquarters in Munich, was cordoned off by army troops assigned to protect Hitler during the "Night of the Long Knives" in 1934. The soldiers attracted little attention from members of the public, who were unaware that Ernst Röhm and the rest of the Brownshirt leadership had just been slaughtered on Hitler's express orders.

of the *Geheimes Staatspolizeiamt* (Prussian Secret State Police Office). Under Himmler's leadership (a frightening mixture of bloodthirstiness and bureaucracy) the secret police soon became notorious as the *Gestapo*. In his new position, Himmler became "Hitler's eyes and ears"—perhaps the most dreaded man in the nation. The nickname of this mild little clerk with rimless glasses was "the Butcher."

Playing one member of his staff off against another was a method by which Hitler protected himself against possible rivals. The government, too, while not prepared to outlaw the organization, desperately wanted the SA reduced, because it had come to represent a potential threat to the small standing army allowed to Germany under the terms of the Treaty of Versailles. The simple soldier Röhm was no match for the devious, fanatically devoted Himmler. With Göring (who had left the SA in the aftermath of the 1923 putsch) and a few other party faithfuls, Himmler began methodically to compile a list of SA members and others in the party to be liquidated. As they explained later, the health of the Nazi party needed a "blood purge." On the night of June 30, 1934—the "Night of the Long Knives"—more than 1,000 of Röhm's men were rounded up and summarily slaughtered. The execution squads worked so fast that few of the victims knew what was happening. Some SA men, arrested in bed with their boyfriends, hustled to jail, and shot within hours, died saluting and calling out "Heil Hitler." The German army—along with Hitler—felt it was a regrettable but necessary action.

President Hindenburg, by now 87 years old, was confused by news of the bloodbath. On August 1 he addressed Hitler as "Your Majesty." The next day he was dead, and Hitler assumed the title of president as well as chancellor.

In 1934, to make clear his absolute control over every element of government, he suggested that he be accorded the new, simple title of *Führer* (Leader)—reflecting, like so many other aspects of Nazism, that its inspiration came from the terminology of Italian fascism. Mussolini's title was *Il Duce*, liter-

The *autobahn* (highway) near Kreuzburg, East Prussia. Hitler's economic recovery program included construction of a system of scenic highways and factories that would build efficient *Volkswagens* (people's cars).

ally also "The Leader." When these proposals were put to a vote, 90% of the public backed them enthusiastically, thus proving that Hitler was undoubtedly the most popular man in Germany at that time.

Also beyond dispute is the fact that he accomplished much of what he had promised. Hitler's reforms were sweeping and largely successful, solving many of the greatest problems of the country. Within just three years of Hitler's becoming chancellor national income doubled, unemployment all but disappeared, and production soared by over a third.

Despite Hitler's ghastly official bloodletting the many Germans who measured their country's history exclusively in terms of its more glorious periods saw the early years of his rule as an auspicious start to the new era which the Führer had promised them.

The Holy Roman Empire, which had lasted from 962 to 1806, was considered the first German *Reich*, or empire. In 1871 Otto von Bismarck, the German statesman known as the "Iron Chancellor," had established an empire which lasted until Germany's defeat in 1918—the Second Reich. In 1933 Hitler, with his sure instinct for the German love of grand gestures, had proclaimed the beginning of

With Eva Braun on the terrace of his Berchtesgaden country house, Hitler plays with Eva's Scotch terriers. Hitler was always fond of dogs but, concerned that such pictures might soften his forceful image, rarely permitted himself to be photographed with them.

the Third Reich. The first had lasted 844 years, the second a mere 47. The glorious Third Reich, Hitler promised, was to last one thousand years.

For a while it seemed that his prophecy might be fulfilled. Indeed, Germany's recovery was stupendous. Hitler claimed that the long-awaited rearmament of the country was the solution to unemployment, giving the people work and the country might at the same time. It now appears, however, that this was largely propaganda, and that the Nazi government actually spent far less on airplanes and submarines than Hitler claimed.

Recovery in Germany really came, as it did in the United States, mainly from massive public works programs—the construction of an enormous network of superhighways, for example, which in turn encouraged the growth of an automobile industry. The road building employed nearly 750,000 men, and the motor factories it stimulated provided work for 1.5 million more.

The grand public buildings, deliberately designed to compete with the Great Pyramid of Egypt, both gave work to the unemployed and fed the country's sense of importance. During the early and mid-1930s, Hitler indulged his wildest dreams of splendor, outdoing his earlier spectacles. Having no real human relationships of any significance Hitler lavished all his feeling on public show. His chief architect, Albert Speer, observed that the only thing that inspired human emotion in Hitler was his dog!

But if he was incapable of loving another human being, Hitler could express his passions in giant political rallies. In fact, the perversion of human emotion which these rallies represented, encouraged, and exploited was probably best understood by Speer himself.

Albert Speer, the archetypal Nazi bureaucrat, came from an old and respected family of master builders. He first caught the attention of the Nazi hierarchy in 1933 when he supervised the technical details for what turned out to be a very successful rally in Berlin. Speer demonstrated, in his orchestration of these spectacles, a grasp of mass psy-

> *The anti-Semitism of reason, however, must lead to the systematic combatting and elimination of Jewish privileges. Its ultimate goal must implacably be the total removal of the Jews. Of both these purposes only a government of national strength is capable, never a government of national impotence.*
> —ADOLF HITLER

chology as profound as Hitler's. In his capable hands Hitler's vision became reality. The walls of flags, the astonishing light shows—all these were the creation of Albert Speer, the kind of artist and architect that Hitler, with his inflated estimation of his own abilities, once said he might have become but for the outbreak of World War I. In the context of the National Socialist state, Speer was a perfect professional. He worked for the state while claiming that its politics had nothing to do with him.

It cannot be denied, however, that Speer was a brilliant administrator. He drove himself to the limit in his search for, as he put it, the "right way" to increase efficiency and overcome seemingly insurmountable obstacles. He was committed to finding the "expert's" answers to the problems created by the morally bankrupt regime for which he worked. While the Nazi rank and file had only patriotism as their pretext for blind obedience to the will of a madman, Speer excused himself on the grounds that he was acting only in a "professional" capacity.

The assessment of Speer given by historian Joachim C. Fest places this gifted but essentially guilty man in a useful perspective: "[Speer represented] a type without which neither the National Socialist nor any other variety of modern totalitarianism could have succeeded: the expert who sought to guarantee himself an irreproachable existence by retreating into the ostensibly unpolitical position of his profession. . . . Men like Speer did not do enough to prevent the establishment and spread of violence; they are open to the reproach of having refused to accept responsibility for what was going on. For a plea of duty amounts to very little in a state where uniforms are worn, acts of violence performed, and people arrested and killed."

The great Nazi rallies of the 1930s were attended by hundreds of thousands, all stirred to an almost demonic fever of excitement by the theatrical staging of the event. A circle of searchlights in the grandstands aimed great shafts of light to a central point above the field. In this "cathedral of light" the Führer solemnly marched at the head of a great procession to the podium. One witness reported that: "Thunderous cheers drowned the music of the massed bands playing him in. He ascended . . . and stood there waiting until there was complete silence. Then suddenly there appeared far in the distance a mass of advancing red color. It was the 25,000 banners of the Nazi organizations."

In some ways, however, it often seemed that the public Adolf Hitler, the earthshaking speaker and leader at the center of all this magnificently excessive spectacle, bore little relation to the prim and distant man who emerged in private when the parades were over and the searchlights no longer stabbed into the sky. Hitler tended to fuss around his office, forever rearranging things on his desk and badgering his staff about smoking or eating the wrong foods. He was a vegetarian who never smoked or drank, but stuffed himself with chocolate, ate huge quantities of cake, and took seven spoonfuls of sugar in his tea. Such mundane personal characteristics hardly suggested the presence of a man who would shortly bring death and devastation to millions.

To many outside observers, however, and to those Germans whose independence of mind had saved them from becoming completely caught up in the new national awareness, Hitler's dark side was readily apparent and constituted immense cause for concern. They realized that his seizure of power at home was only the beginning and that his concept of a Third Reich, a "Greater Germany" he was to restore to its heroic and glorious position of supremacy in Europe, would eventually, and inevitably, involve carrying the National Socialist revolution beyond the Fatherland's present borders.

In 1933 a diminutive figure with the comical name of Engelbert Dollfuss had seized power in Austria. American humorist Will Rogers had quipped of this tiny dictator that he was "so small they can't assassinate him because if they miss him they'll shoot themselves in the foot." In 1934, however, Dollfuss was assassinated and Germany immediately attempted to take control of Austria in

Hitler and Albert Speer (1905-1981) in 1937. Later appointed minister of armaments, Speer had just been named general architectural inspector. He was to be responsible, said Hitler, for turning Berlin into "a true capital of the German Reich." At the war's end, Speer received a 20-year prison sentence.

Backed by a monolithic display of swastikas, Hitler addresses laborers at Berlin's Tempelhof airport in 1934. Hitler and other high Nazi party officials always made a point of appearing in awe-inspiring, highly theatrical settings.

the midst of the confusion that followed the shooting. Due to Italian diplomatic intervention, however, Hitler's bid for Germany's southern neighbor failed. But people were beginning to notice his plans. When he announced in 1935 that he was establishing a universal draft to build a German army and air force, it was clear that he had "torn up the Versailles Treaty," as the newspapers of America and England put it. "It wasn't a good treaty," an American commentator observed, "but it was the only one they had." Britain and France protested, but Hitler got away with it. He rightly guessed that the Allies, nearly 20 years after the previous war, would not put themselves on the line to oppose a growing Germany.

The attempt to overrun Austria and the open development of an army were only two of the clues that Hitler gave to his ambitions. He had never made any secret of his dream of a Greater German empire stretching eastward across Europe, swallowing up any country that stood in its way. *Mein Kampf* contained clear hints of it, and Hitler's speeches never ceased to harp on Germany's glorious imperial destiny.

Many Americans saw him as a gangster. "A guy named Hitler has Germany like Capone has Chicago," Will Rogers said. The English considered him a vulgar, common little man with ridiculous delusions of grandeur. With all the evidence to the contrary swelling obscenely before their eyes, many Europeans continued to believe that he was nothing to take too seriously. They often dismissed the success of this strutting little demagogue with the Charlie Chaplin moustache as something of an aberration in German politics and unlikely to last. They also imagined that he would be easy to control if he ever tried to get tough.

But Hitler had always been tough, with the capacity for endurance and indifference to danger and pain which distinguishes the true fanatic from the mere self-promoter. As a matter of fact, Hitler was exceptionally brave in the face of physical pain. He could put himself into a trance in which he felt nothing. When he had dental surgery after taking office as chancellor, he amazed his staff by sitting stone-faced through the whole operation without an anesthetic.

A similar spirit of disregard for suffering, be it his own or another's, pervaded his public stance. From his earliest youth he had an all-or-nothing attitude, and often displayed a readiness to stake everything on a single gamble. He seemed impervious to the probable consequences of failure. On more than one occasion he remarked that, if the Nazi party fell, it would bring the world down with it.

The success of his programs for economic recovery made his position unassailable and his popularity incomparable. He saw himself as a man of destiny, and many Germans had come to share his vision. Step by step, he set about implementing the rest of his plans.

The task which I have to fulfill is an unpolitical one. I felt comfortable in my work so long as my person and also my work were valued solely according to my specialist achievement.
—ALBERT SPEER
in a memorandum to Hitler

Hitler reviews a parade of goose-stepping German Labor Service members. The Labor Service was part of the training system for young men that began with the *Jungvolk* and Hitler Youth and ended with the military—the *Wehrmacht*.

8
The Empire-Builder

If Hitler's thoughts can be compared to the music of a symphony by Wagner, then the central and constantly recurring theme was surely his dream of a Greater German empire, a unified superstate of all German-speaking lands. He had gained a glimpse of how such a union might have looked when Germany and Austria had fought as allies during World War I and then witnessed the shattering of this prospect when the Treaty of Versailles forbade any political continuation of what had originally been a military alliance. As the iron grip of the treaty began to relax, however, Hitler's thoughts turned increasingly to expansion.

Among his first actions in 1933 were cautious efforts at the rearmament of Germany. Although his speeches exaggerated its extent, he did what he could to build an army and an air force. The failure of the Nazi effort to seize Austria in 1934 constituted only a temporary setback for Hitler, and he began wholesale conscription of soldiers the very next year. By 1936 he felt sufficiently confident to offer his first direct challenge to the Allied powers and the terms of the treaty with which they had humiliated Germany in 1919. He sent two divisions of troops into the Rhineland, the area west of the Rhine River where the Allies had forbidden Germany to station troops.

> *The chief function [of propaganda] is to convince the masses, whose slowness of understanding needs to be given time in order that they may absorb information; and only constant repetition will finally succeed in imprinting an idea on their mind.*
> —ADOLF HITLER

Saarlanders celebrating their reunion with Germany in 1935. The Saar, a coal-rich industrial region on the Franco-German border, had been stripped from Germany following World War I. After an intense Nazi propaganda campaign, however, its residents enthusiastically and overwhelmingly voted to join the Third Reich.

Hitler, speaking beneath a mammoth German eagle on a swastika, broadcasts a speech urging voter ratification of the annexation of Austria. Popular support for the move was overwhelming: 99% of the voters in both Germany and Austria strongly approved.

American athlete Jesse Owens (1913–1980) shows the form that won him four gold medals in the 1936 Olympic Games. Hitler, who had congratulated earlier winners, refused to shake hands with Owens because he was black.

The Allies had demanded that the region remain demilitarized in order to enhance the security of the French border in the event of future German aggression. The French were naturally alarmed at Hitler's move. The return of German troops to the Rhineland nagged at their memories of the ease and speed with which the German offensive of 1914 had burst upon them before they had the slightest chance to estimate its size and direction.

The government in Paris protested, but received no support. British foreign affairs chiefs thought it no business of theirs what the Germans did in their own country, and Italy was eager to maintain good relations with Germany. The government of the United States, grappling with severe economic problems, had no wish to get involved in a dispute it considered entirely a European affair.

Thus Hitler's first aggressive move—as clear a statement of his intentions as anyone could ask for—met with complete success and went largely unheeded by many nations which eventually would discover the high price of conducting foreign policy on the basis of short-sightedness and indifference.

Although no government actually opposed Hitler, he had little European backing. His only ally was Mussolini, who had his own dreams of glory to pursue. Italy's support was valuable to Hitler, and he greatly prized the personal good will of its leader.

Benito Mussolini was a tough, aggressive politician with high ambitions and a somewhat clearer head than Hitler's. This former journalist's charismatic eloquence and romantic promises of a return to the glory of ancient Rome had gained him the position of uncontested dictator of Italy in 1922. He had fired the hopes of the poor and hungry in that desperate country as Hitler did in Germany 11 years later. Mussolini too created giant public works projects and built great highways. His greatest boast was that he made the Italian trains run on time.

Hitler had learned and borrowed much from Il Duce and had come to regard him as a role model. If the strutting and ranting Italian sometimes appeared slightly ridiculous, he clearly knew what he was doing. Mussolini, although privately dismis-

sive of the Germans, recognized their growing influence and knew—or thought he knew—where his own best interests lay. He was not as passionate a fanatic as Hitler; he was a calm opportunist who gambled only on what he considered the surest of bets. In October 1936, believing that one day they would control the entire continent of Europe, the two men formed an alliance. They envisaged the rest of Europe radiating from the line between their two capitals, and called that line the Rome-Berlin Axis. The "Axis powers" were soon to rock the world.

Mussolini and Hitler both wanted the same thing: more land. The Germans called it *Lebensraum* (living space). Mussolini wanted to make the Mediterranean Sea an Italian lake and sought to surround it by seizing territory in Africa. In 1935 he launched a full-scale air, land, and sea invasion of the ancient and independent African kingdom of Ethiopia.

When the League of Nations protested, Italy simply left the organization. Hitler found the precedent established by Mussolini distinctly encouraging. If the Italian dictator could indulge his taste for foreign adventurism and emerge unscathed, could not he, Adolf Hitler, expect to conduct German foreign policy with similar impunity?

In 1938 Hitler decided his support in Austria was great enough to force the issue. For years he had dreamed of *Anschluss* (political union) with Austria, the other Germanic nation. Backed by well-organized Nazi demonstrations, he pressured Kurt von Schuschnigg, the Austrian chancellor, to give the Austrian Nazi party official recognition and to appoint Nazis to important government posts. When Schuschnigg called for a public vote on the matter, Hitler sent troops in at once and occupied the land of his birth.

At last Hitler had the pleasure of returning to Vienna, where he had had such a hard and lonely life, in triumph. The Nazis there received him rapturously, welcoming the *Anschluss* and fully believing that Hitler, far from conquering the country, had simply opened the doors of the Reich to one of its children. Not only was the Greater German empire becoming a reality, but Hitler was achieving it, as he had expected, with even less opposition from the Allies than had been forthcoming following the occupation of the Rhineland. Also ominous was the speed with which the SS and Gestapo put Nazi social policies into effect in Austria. Many foreign observers remarked that what had taken years in Germany took just weeks in Austria. Hitler's annexation of his native land established the pattern that future invasions would follow. In the wake of the troops would come the New Order, the mythology of race supremacy, the concentration camps for Jews and intellectuals, and the crushing of all political opposition.

That was in February 1938. Things were now moving fast for Hitler and his party. It became increasingly clear that further expansionist moves would encounter little or no opposition, and he seized the chance to press yet another territorial claim. In the summer of 1938 he demanded the return of the Sudetenland.

This strip bordering Czechoslovakia had been taken from Germany under the terms of the Treaty of Versailles. Its loss had rankled the Germans ever since, not simply because the area was historically German and rich in natural resources, but also because the Sudeten Germans had for many years been the dominant population group in the region. The rise of Germany was fast becoming a fact of political life in Europe, and, while other countries recognized the seriousness of the situation, none was prepared to risk a direct confrontation.

In September 1938 British and French representatives arrived in Germany to try to work out a peaceful solution to the problem. In Munich they made Hitler an offer he simply could not resist. If he would agree not to invade Czechoslovakia, their

Solemn children present flowers to a smiling Adolf Hitler in Vienna following the German annexation of Austria. Hitler was delighted to return as Führer to the country where he had once been just an unemployed artist.

governments would support his claim to the Sudetenland. He had faced the world down and gotten what he wanted without firing a shot. As he had foreseen, Britain and France were now too intimidated to risk a showdown.

Britain's Prime Minister Neville Chamberlain was a steady but basically uninspired politician known for his caution and often accused by opponents and colleagues alike of lacking perception. Generally considered an intellectual featherweight, this well-meaning but ineffectual premier became a hero overnight in his own country.

He returned to Britain clutching a scrap of paper supposedly containing the terms of a new treaty and boasting that he had secured "peace in our time"—a phrase that was to haunt him for the rest of his life. His achievement had been to sign away part of Czechoslovakia in order to appease the bully of Berlin. Chamberlain had not allowed his judgment to be influenced by the inconvenient fact that France, Britain's closest ally, was supposedly committed by treaty to aid Czechoslovakia in the event of invasion. His conscience was no doubt considerably eased by the fact that France too had chosen to forget this particular commitment.

Hitler was overjoyed. He had seen that Britain and France would not fight to support their allies. He had staked everything and won. Now, with the Sudetenland under his control, the rest of Czechoslovakia would be easy prey. Throughout the following year, Hitler repeatedly flouted the Munich agreements.

German propaganda encouraged disaffection among Czechoslovakia's minorities, forcing the government to grant self-rule to several regions. Under pressure from Berlin, Slovakia declared independence on March 14, 1939. Early in the morning of March 15, Hitler forced the Czech government to allow the provinces of Bohemia and Moravia to become German protectorates. Thus, just six months after declaring that all he wanted was the Sudetenland, Hitler had wiped Czechoslovakia from the map of Europe without recourse to open warfare, employing nothing but skillful intimidation. Hitler

From his country home in Berchtesgaden, Hitler had a clear view of Austria, which he had long dreamed of incorporating into a Greater Germany. He got what he wanted in 1938, when Nazi armored divisions rumbled across the Austro-German border.

Hitler hands out autographs at the 1936 Olympic Games in Berlin. To placate international teams and foreign visitors to the games, Hitler ordered the temporary removal of anti-Semitic posters and permitted a few Jewish athletes to represent the Reich. After the Games anti-Semitism became more intense.

Soviet communist dictator Joseph Stalin (1879-1953) shocked the West when he signed a nonaggression treaty with German fascist dictator Adolf Hitler. Soon after the pact was signed, Hitler invaded Poland.

British prime minister (Arthur) Neville Chamberlain (1869-1940) and Hitler met in 1938 to discuss German intentions toward Czechoslovakia. Hitler told Chamberlain that his demand for Czech territory was "the last which he had to make in Europe." Chamberlain made the fatal mistake of believing the wily and devious Nazi leader.

had known all along that he would meet no opposition from France or Britain, Czechoslovakia's supposedly loyal allies. "I saw those worms at Munich," he later sneered.

The world stood by, watching Hitler swallow pieces of Europe, and did nothing. The United States maintained a policy of isolationism and contented itself with repeatedly issuing useless statements which expressed disapproval of Germany and sympathy with its victims.

Although the destruction of Czechoslovakia must have seemed an unqualified triumph to Hitler, the fact that the ambassadors of Britain and France delivered the protests of their respective governments to Berlin actually indicated that Hitler's days of easy conquests were numbered. Public support for appeasement in those two countries evaporated just days after the Germans marched into Prague. From that point on, British and French foreign policy took increasing account of growing public hostility toward Germany.

Following his bloodless triumphs in Austria and Czechoslovakia, Hitler turned his attention toward the territories that had always figured most prominently in his plans for expanding the Reich—Poland and the other states of eastern Europe. The success of any German action in this direction would depend not only upon adequate military capacity but also upon effective prior diplomacy. Hitler needed a negotiator who could buy Germany sufficient political insurance abroad to enable it to conduct a major operation without triggering a major war. Hitler believed he had found such a man in Joachim von Ribbentrop.

A somewhat younger man who had joined the party in 1932, Ribbentrop had an advantage over most of Hitler's advisors, and over Hitler himself. He was a man of the world. His education and his work as a wine merchant had taken him to France and the United States. As a result he knew two more languages than most members of the Nazi inner circle. He was not a particularly shrewd diplomat, but, like many of the party faithful, what he lacked in intelligence he made up for in loyalty.

After two years as ambassador to England, he became Germany's foreign minister in 1938. He helped engineer the absorption of Austria and Czechoslovakia into the Reich, and had played a modest part in negotiating the alliance with Italy in 1936. The most important diplomatic negotiations presided over by Ribbentrop were those which resulted in the nonaggression pact concluded between Nazi Germany and the Soviet Union in August 1939. Ribbentrop was seeking political insurance with a vengeance at this point. Hitler's most daring move to date, the invasion of Poland, was just days away, and even the German-Japanese anticommunist pact of 1936 did not disturb Ribbentrop's calculations.

The invasion of Poland was the end to which all Hitler's advocacy of expansion had pointed. Every public action of the party since he had taken office had prepared the nation for it. Constantly, his propaganda machine had pounded the concept of *Lebensraum* into the heads of the German people.

His minister of propaganda and public enlightenment, Joseph Goebbels, had asserted in 1936 that "War is the most simple affirmation of life." Goebbels was one of the most sinister men in the entire gallery of misfits surrounding the Führer. Born with a clubfoot, this "lame, lop-eared, loose-mouthed little man," as one American commentator described him, was the only senior official of the Nazi party who might have been more cold-blooded and anti-Semitic than Himmler or even Hitler. It is always difficult to assess accurately the extent of a particular individual's influence on the collective decisions which translate into government policy. Some of the most horrifying policies of the Nazi party, however, can be traced to Joseph Goebbels. Hitler inspired and ordered the notorious "final solution to the Jewish question." Himmler's SS provided the criminals in uniform who would perform the dreadful work, and a Gestapo officer named Adolf Eichmann took care of the administrative details. But it was the quiet, methodical, highly educated Dr. Goebbels who defined it. According to historian Robert Herzstein, "Goebbels had all along been the one high Nazi leader

Jackbooted members of the German-American *Bund* (league) on parade with U.S. and Nazi flags in New York City in 1937. The Bund openly proclaimed its strong pro-Hitler sentiments up to the moment when the United States declared war on Nazi Germany in December of 1941.

Jeder Groschen
für unsere Presse-

Ein Schlag
in diese Lügenpresse!

The German anti-Nazi underground published this cartoon of Joseph Goebbels (1897-1945), captioned "Every penny for our press is a kick in this liar's face."

The forty-eight hours after the march were the most nerve-wracking in my life. . . . Good Lord, I'm relieved how smoothly everything went! Yes, the world belongs to the courageous man. God helps him.

—ADOLF HITLER
speaking after the German remilitarization of the Rhineland in 1936

who had insisted upon the necessity of actually *exterminating* the Jews."

Goebbels was a master of propaganda, a skilled showman who boasted that he could make the public believe anything. Convinced, like his Führer, that Germany needed *Lebensraum,* he devoted himself to preparing the German people to fight for it.

The hour had struck, he told them, for Germany to assert its historic claim in Europe. The high destiny of the Master Race was at hand. They must be willing to sacrifice themselves for the glory of the Reich. Every comfort must give way to the need for arms.

"Guns before butter" became the Goebbels rallying cry. Although he lived in lavish surroundings on his great estate, Goebbels hammered away at preaching the need for Germans to do without luxuries. From now on, they would be living within the constrictions of a war economy. All production would work in one direction only, and have but one aim—to rebuild the army. "We can do without butter," he said in a speech in 1936, "but not without arms. One cannot shoot with butter, but with guns." Even Göring, now the head of the air force and often in conflict with the propaganda minister, backed him on this point. The air marshal, now obese and notorious for his grossly self-indulgent, almost princely life style, made the same point in a radio speech that year. Despite the fact that his own bloated physique was no great advertisement for an austerity program, he said, "Guns will make us powerful, butter will only make us fat."

Although German rearmament had made much progress by 1939, there was one power which Hitler knew he could not afford to fight for some time yet—the Soviet Union. Any German military action in eastern Europe would be doomed to failure if communist dictator Joseph Stalin's military and economic superstate became involved.

The nonaggression pact concluded between Germany and the Soviet Union in August 1939 was the turning point for Hitler. No longer haunted by the fear of Soviet retaliation, he could make his move against Poland. He did not want a world war—indeed, Germany was not in any position to fight a war on such a scale. He only wanted a piece of Poland to add to his growing German empire. The pact with Stalin guaranteed that the Soviets would not oppose the move. In fact, the understanding was that Germany and the Soviet Union would carve Poland up between them. Germany had also agreed to take no action in the event of a Soviet invasion of Finland.

Hitler was hopeful that Britain and France would give Poland no more help than they had given Czechoslovakia. He expected further carefully worded protests and nothing more. Ultimately, he hoped for an alliance with the leading European maritime power, Great Britain, which would guarantee his country's supremacy on the Continent. Once Poland fell, he was sure, the world would accept this latest conquest as it had accepted Germany's *Anschluss* with Austria and the dismemberment of Czechoslovakia.

The pact with the Soviet Union was signed on August 23, 1939. Two days later Franklin D. Roosevelt, president of the United States, sent an appeal to Hitler to settle his demands on Poland peacefully. Hitler simply ignored him. Five days later, on September 1, 1939, Germany launched a full-scale invasion of Poland.

It started just after midnight with massed dive bombers raining destruction on railroads, highways, factories, and cities. Working to a strict timetable, armored forces smashed through the hastily assembled Polish formations, clearing the way for columns of infantry. It was possibly the best-planned, fastest, and most efficiently fought military action of modern times. *Blitzkrieg* (lightning war) was the term which Germany's war planners used to describe the revolutionary tactics they had developed and first used in Poland.

Two days later, on September 3, Hitler's worst fears were realized when France and England honored their commitments to Poland and declared war on Germany. Appeasement was a thing of the past. World War II had begun.

> *Further successes can no longer be attained without the shedding of blood. . . . It is a question of expanding our living space in the east . . . . There is no question of sparing Poland and we are left with the decision: To attack Poland at the first suitable opportunity.*
> —ADOLF HITLER
> speaking to his senior officers in 1939

Paving the way for the invasion of Poland—and for World War II—*Luftwaffe* (Air Force) bombers roar eastward out of Germany. By the time Poland fell, a mere 19 days later, Europe was a continent at war.

9

The Victor

On September 17 Stalin's soldiers marched into Poland from the east, as planned. They encountered little resistance since the bulk of Poland's armed forces had already succumbed to the savage German onslaught. Poland had fallen so quickly that Britain and France had no time to mount an effective military response. Stalin and Hitler divided the spoils, Germany taking the rich industrial areas in the western part of the country and Russia the eastern third. Stalin did not mind the unequal division because the same pact that had assured Hitler of Soviet support in Poland also guaranteed Stalin Germany's support for his seizure of Finland and the Baltic states—Estonia, Latvia, and Lithuania.

Encouraged by the success of the Polish campaign, the strength of the alliance with Italy, and the guarantee of Soviet neutrality, Hitler felt he could safely contemplate moving against the nations of western Europe. He also considered it a good time in which to turn his attention to his own country, where most Germans were gloating over their easy triumphs. The forging of a German empire seemed to be off to a good start.

But the German empire was only one of the two great themes of Hitler's life. The other was racial purity, the "cleansing" of his country of inferior

Shouting "Sieg Heil! Heil Hitler!" thousands of Germans greet Hitler with a massive Nazi salute. The appearance of their Führer often excited crowds to displays of mass hysteria.

Perched on the steps of his country home, Hitler wears the traditional costume of the Tyrol, the Alpine region of western Austria. In 1939, with Poland defeated, Mussolini on his side, and Stalin promising not to interfere with the expansion of his empire, Hitler could afford to be both relaxed and optimistic.

Robed students cheer as the flames of a bonfire consume books in Berlin. Book burnings commenced with works by Jewish authors, but soon all "un-German" books—including those written by such famous authors as Jack London and Helen Keller—were consigned to the flames.

elements. This purification—Hitler often referred to it in medical terms, such as "disinfection"—had already begun. Among Hitler's first moves as chancellor, in 1933, was the disenfranchisement of Jews—taking away their right to vote.

The roots of Hitler's obsession with seeking "a final solution to the Jewish question" go back much deeper into the past. Hitler's anti-Semitism was well established back in Vienna, and in 1922 he had made his intentions clear to a friend when he said: "If I am ever really in power, the destruction of the Jews will be my first and most important job. . . . I will have gallows erected . . . as many of them as the traffic allows. Then the Jews will be hanged, and they will stay hanging until they stink."

In 1935 the Nuremberg Laws forbade Germans to marry or do business with Jews, and reclassed Jews as "subjects" rather than citizens. Books by or sympathetic to Jews were already being publicly burned. "The past is lying in flames," cried Dr. Goebbels at one such book burning. "The future will rise from the flames within our hearts. . . . These flames light up a new era."

Further legislation made life increasingly hard for Jews in Germany, and many—mainly those who could afford to do so—emigrated. But Jews were well established in that country, and most doubted that the Hitler regime would last very long. Indeed, Germany's Jewish population was probably the best-assimilated in the world. Unlike their coreligionists in eastern Europe, German Jews had enjoyed full rights of citizenship until the Nazis came to power. They had acquired both prominence and respect in many fields—government, finance, law, medicine, the arts, and even the profession of arms. Many German Jews had marched, fought, and died for the Fatherland during World War I.

With a record of public service and patriotic devotion such as this, it is, perhaps, not surprising that not until 1938 did the extremity of their danger become fully apparent to the Jews of Germany. By then, however, it was too late for many of them.

On the night of November 9, 1938, two days after a young German Jew had protested Nazi anti-

Semitic policies by shooting a German diplomat in Paris, Goebbels arranged for retaliatory "spontaneous" demonstrations against the Jews all over the country. Homes were wrecked, stores looted, synagogues burned, and people killed. The shattered windows that filled the streets gave the event its name, *Kristallnacht* ("Crystal Night" or "The Night of Broken Glass").

The barbarism continued throughout November 10, while the police stood by and watched or directed traffic around the disturbances as gangs demolished the Jewish communities of Germany. The official report admits to 814 shops, 171 homes, and 191 synagogues destroyed. About 90 people were murdered and when it was over, the police arrested 20,000 Jews and shipped them to concentration camps. As a final insult, the remaining Jews were fined 1 billion marks—for damages! A German diplomat reported that Hitler "squealed with delight and slapped his thigh with enthusiasm" when he received the report.

Early in 1939 Hitler made a speech in which he declared that in a world subject to the Nazi social order the Jewish race in Europe would be eliminated. Following the invasion of Poland, thousands of that country's Jews were relocated in urban areas that had been designated as ghettos. The practice of confinement did not turn into a policy of systematic killing until 1941, when Germany invaded the Soviet Union.

In December 1940, shortly after signing the orders for this invasion, Hitler had instructed Himmler and Reinhard Heydrich, the head of the security service, to make preparations for a "final solution" to the Jewish "question." As the Wehrmacht geared up for the invasion during the first six months of 1941, thousands of SS troopers were formed into units called *Einsatzgruppen* (Special Action Squads). Smaller forerunners of these special forces had first been employed in Poland, where they had methodically murdered the majority of that country's intelligentsia.

Germany invaded the Soviet Union on June 22, 1941, and the *Einsatzgruppen* went into action

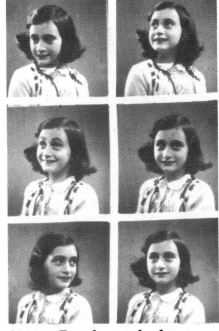

Anne Frank and her family—German Jews who spent two years hiding from the Nazis in an Amsterdam attic—were finally arrested in 1944. Anne was 15 when she died in the Nazi death camp at Bergen-Belsen. Her secret diary, published after the war, brought the Holocaust sharply into focus for millions around the world.

German troops round up Jewish men, women, and children in Warsaw, Poland, for deportation to the killing centers. In 1943 the Warsaw ghetto's few surviving Jews decided to resist. Virtually unarmed, they held off German troops, tanks, and flame throwers for almost a month. The SS finally burned the entire ghetto.

just days later. Their orders were to kill every Jew they could find in the occupied territories. Within six months they murdered approximately 600,000 Soviet and Romanian Jews—and yet Hitler and his lieutenants were far from satisfied. They felt that, judging by the performance to date, the *Einsatzgruppen* alone would not suffice to rid Europe of the enemies of the Master Race.

Finally, in 1942, the systematic destruction of European Jewry began in earnest. The policy of deliberate mass murder became known as the Holocaust—or "wholesale burning." Its goal was nothing less than genocide—the killing of a whole people. Hitler had been calling for it, directly or indirectly, publicly or privately, most of his life.

Now he was in a position to take positive action. He saw himself as a doctor lancing a boil or an exterminator going after cockroaches. In fact, the German word for cockroach or vermin was often applied to Jews in Nazi propaganda.

Anti-Semitism had had a long history in Europe, but it had never led to anything on the scale of the cold and methodical system of mass murder created by the government of Nazi Germany. By 1942 many concentration camps had been set up, mostly in the German-occupied territories of central and eastern Europe. Along with vast numbers of Jews, the camps also housed Gypsies (another inferior people according to Nazi racial theories), Catholics,

communists, and political dissidents.

In mid-March of that year the first camp designed specifically for methodical mass murder became operational. At Belzec, in Poland, Jews transported from the ghetto in Lublin were crowded into an airtight bunker and gassed to death. Two other camps whose names continue to haunt the conscience of mankind, Sobibor and Treblinka, commenced operations a few months later.

Those too weak to work on the forced-labor projects were killed immediately. No one was spared. Women, children, and the aged were usually the first to die. With horrifying efficiency, studies were made and experiments conducted by German scientists to find the most efficient and inexpensive ways of killing and disposing of millions of human beings.

Another ghastly aspect of this crime against humanity was that the extermination became a business. Himmler, the Nazis' chief executioner, turned the camps into factories which made soap from the bodies of murdered Jews. A special iron hook was designed for tearing open the mouths of the dead to find gold in their teeth. Women's hair was cut off to make slippers for submarine crews, and babies whose crying bothered the guards were smashed against the wall.

By the end of 1942, according to an SS report, 2.5 million Jews had been transported to various

> *The [eastern European races] are to work for us. In so far as we do not need them, they may die. [Their] fertility is undesirable. Education is dangerous. We shall leave them religion as a means of diversion. They will receive only the absolutely necessary provisions. We are the masters, we come first.*
> —MARTIN BORMANN
> Hitler's deputy

> *Never again must the churches be allowed any influence over the leadership of the people. This must be broken totally and forever. Only then will the existence of nation and Reich be assured.*
> —MARTIN BORMANN
> Hitler's deputy

The bodies of murdered concentration camp inmates lie stacked like firewood at Bergen-Belsen. Throughout the war most Germans knew that the nation's Jews were being persecuted, but few were reportedly aware of the ghastly scale of the killing.

This doorway at the Dachau concentration camp is marked "showerbath," but it led to a gas chamber. Prisoners were crowded together and killed by poison gas pouring from vents in the ceiling. The bodies were burned in nearby ovens.

camps and killed. The victims had come from Germany, the Sudetenland, Austria, Bohemia, Moravia, Poland, France, the Netherlands, Belgium, Norway, and the Soviet Union. Only in one European country were Hitler's plans for the deportation of Jews successfully thwarted. The resistance forces in occupied Denmark, aided by thousands of ordinary citizens, conducted an undercover evacuation of the country's Jewish community to neutral Sweden. This effort, however, even when combined with those of the many individual Europeans who sheltered Jews from their persecutors, saved but a few thousand souls from Hitler's genocidal obsession.

The killing went on until the very end of the war, when it was obvious that Germany had lost. Hitler never gave up his dream of "cleansing" Europe of Jews. Men and equipment desperately needed at the battlefront were transferred, at Hitler's personal orders, to the death camps to keep the ovens burning. Even in his will Hitler left his money to his family, his personal effects to his party, and to his country the command: "Continue to fight the Jews."

The emaciated body of a Bergen-Belsen inmate offers horrifying evidence of the Nazi program of genocide. Deliberate starvation was among the methods selected by the SS to murder every Jew in Europe.

The grisly sight of crematoriums filled with the bones of murdered prisoners greeted those American troops who liberated the Buchenwald concentration camp in 1945. Four million of the six million Jews killed by the Nazis died at camps like Buchenwald.

The war went well for Hitler at first. He had not really armed Germany for the long, large-scale struggle he had brought about by invading Poland, but he had a head start on all the other nations that were drawn into it. In April 1940 the Wehrmacht marched into Denmark and also conducted a successful invasion of Norway by air and sea. Both countries fell almost at once. It seemed that nothing could stop the Germans.

Encouraged, Hitler pushed on westward, and on May 10 invaded Belgium, Luxembourg, and the Netherlands. The next day, Winston Churchill became prime minister of Great Britain in succession to Neville Chamberlain, who had resigned following a parliamentary vote of no-confidence. "I have nothing to offer," Churchill told the British people, "but blood, toil, tears, and sweat."

At first it did not seem to be enough. Hitler had rightly foreseen Britain's naval power as a major obstacle to his ambitions and had built a large fleet of submarines to oppose it. These deadly U-boats were the terror of the Atlantic, striking secretly at British transports and supply boats that lacked the technology to fight their unseen attackers.

The British Expeditionary Force took a severe beating in Belgium and then found itself separated from further reinforcement by the French due to a German armored breakthrough in northeastern France. So successful was this main German blitzkrieg attack that the Allied command structure fell apart in a matter of days. French morale never recovered from the shock and the isolated British contingent had to conduct a fighting retreat to the French coast. Evacuating from the port of Dunkirk, under constant attack from German aircraft and leaving most of their equipment behind, the British forces barely succeeded in escaping annihilation. Dunkirk became a symbol of defeat and retreat.

Without British help, France stood alone. It struggled valiantly, but was no match for the Wehrmacht. On June 22, 1940, the French government agreed to the German terms for an armistice. It was one of the high points of Hitler's life. The surrender was signed at Compiègne—the forest where Germany had surrendered in World War I. Hitler, whose keen sense of theater had not deserted him, greatly enjoyed the irony of the situation. He had smarted under the humiliation of Germany's World War I defeat for 22 years. Revenge was sweet.

Adolf Hitler now stood at the pinnacle of his success. He ruled Europe. Germany had grown from 180,976 to 323,360 square miles and its population from 65 million to nearly 106 million. The Third Reich had become the empire he had always dreamed of!

Only Britain now opposed him. Hitler had often entertained hopes of forming an anti-Soviet alliance with the British, and he renewed his proposal accordingly. But Hitler's contempt for the Munich agreements had made it most unlikely that they would repeat Chamberlain's simpleminded mistake. "You cannot do business with Mr. Hitler" became a popular slogan throughout the country. On July 10 Hitler ordered Göring to begin bombing British ships in the Channel. The British retaliated, and the Battle of Britain—the first major, strategic air war in history—began.

Britain's Royal Air Force was comparatively new and largely untested, with many of its members under 20 years old. Although at the beginning of the battle the Germans had a distinct numerical advantage in both pilots and aircraft, they did not meet with the success they had anticipated. Göring's insane refusal to rotate his aircrews badly damaged Luftwaffe morale and operational efficiency. The technological superiority of Britain's fighters, combined with the RAF's radar-guided interception capability, eventually proved decisive. The RAF fought a sober and careful battle of attrition, successfully stemming the German tide, and winning the admiration and gratitude of the whole population for their heroic resistance against considerable odds. Hitler was reluctantly forced to give up his plans to invade Great Britain. On August 25, 1940, the RAF broke through Germany's air defense system and returned Hitler's favor by bombing Berlin.

The Battle of Britain was a great shock to Hitler,

A triumphant Hitler inspects Nazi-occupied Paris in 1940. "Paris has always fascinated me," he remarked during his tour of the city. Hitler also visited the tomb of Napoleon Bonaparte (1769-1821), a famous soldier and statesman whose military genius he absolutely idolized.

German bombers inflicted immense damage on London during 1940. By the end of the war Britain's civilian casualties stood at 60,000 killed and nearly 90,000 wounded.

who had come to believe that Germany was invincible. It was the first real setback he had suffered and the first significant opposition he had encountered.

Hitler angrily ordered Göring to switch from operations against RAF airfields and concentrate his raids on London, hoping thus to break the spirit of Britain's civilian population. For months, as many as 1,000 bombers, escorted by up to 700 fighter planes, attacked London on a daily basis.

Following Prime Minister Winston Churchill's fearless and pugnacious example the British people remained undaunted. This tough and outspoken politician, son of an English lord and an American socialite, had the face and the spirit of the traditional British bulldog, and his defiant manner consistently inspired his beleaguered compatriots. Britain's policy, he declared emphatically, was "to wage war, by sea and air, with all our might and with all the strength that God gave us: to wage war against a monstrous tyranny, never surpassed in the dark lamentable catalogue of human crime."

Churchill's powerful oratory rallied his people as nothing else could have done. Their valor under pressure became a model for the world. "This was," Churchill asserted, "their finest hour."

The British fought a daring defensive war but were still barely surviving. When, in March 1941, they landed troops in Greece, hoping to establish a new front in the Balkans, the experience of Dunkirk was repeated. Within weeks the British were overwhelmed by superior German forces and barely escaped.

Bulgaria, Romania, and Hungary offered only token resistance as Hitler continued his campaign. Eastern Europe was now solidly under German control. The nonaggression pact with Stalin had served its purpose, and it was time to proceed with the master plan.

The invasion of the Soviet Union would constitute the last act of the drama Hitler had originally sketched out in *Mein Kampf*, the necessary end to which his life's work tended. The communists, Hitler believed, were natural enemies of the Nazis, and the racially inferior Slavs (the ethnic group comprising the majority of the Soviet population) were, like the Jews, the natural enemies of the Master Race. They would have to be destroyed like the Jews if Europe was to be cleansed. The necessity of Hitler's invasion of the Soviet Union was as clear to him and his people as any other element of Germany's search for its national destiny.

Displaying his usual inclination toward superstition, Hitler chose June 22 as a lucky day for his latest and most critical enterprise. On that day one year before, the French had signed the armistice at Compiègne, and June 22, 1812, had been Napoleon's day to invade Russia. It seemed to Hitler a good omen. He was, of course, perfectly aware of the result of Napoleon's attempt—the disastrous retreat from Moscow in the depths of the Russian winter—but he reasoned that the blitzkrieg, with its dive bombers and tanks, would swiftly bring *this* campaign to a favorable conclusion.

And he was almost right. But 1941 held two unwelcome surprises for Hitler that changed the course of history. Two years of victory came to an end, and for the first time Hitler saw the prospect of defeat looming before him. There was no going forward, and no turning back.

On September 11, 1940, the front page of *The New York Times* shows the war's tide beginning to turn: British bombers had struck at the heart of Hitler's empire. Berliners were stunned by the raids on their city, which, Hitler had assured them, would never come under attack.

10
The Vanquished

I feel as though I were pushing open a door into a dark room I had never seen—not knowing what lies beyond the door.
—ADOLF HITLER
speaking shortly after the German invasion of the Soviet Union

The invasion of the Soviet Union was the greatest gamble Hitler had taken yet, but this time, as he would soon discover, his luck had deserted him. The consequences for Germany would prove to be horrifying. By late November of 1941 the Wehrmacht had fought its way to the outskirts of Moscow, and victory still seemed possible despite the fact that the onset of the harshest winter in Russian history had already begun to expose serious flaws in German strategy.

Hitler's men were as unprepared for the cold as Napoleon's had been. The Führer had been convinced that the Soviet Union would capitulate within four to six weeks. No provision had been made for winter clothing for the troops, and aircraft, tank, and truck engines froze solid and cracked in the subzero temperatures. Even the guns froze for want of special cold-weather lubricants. The advance was stalled, the army almost incapable of fighting.

Soviet dictator Joseph Stalin, suspecting that the Germans would eventually find themselves in this position, had ordered a "scorched earth" policy—which meant leaving nothing that the enemy might use. With food supplies exhausted, fuel stocks depleted, and hundreds of troops dying of cold every day, some senior Wehrmacht commanders begged

Hitler seemed to be focusing on his own private version of reality in 1941. His belief that his army was unstoppable and that his empire would last "a thousand years" appeared unshaken even by the disastrous reverses suffered by his overextended Wehrmacht in the Soviet Union.

The faces of these German soldiers reflect the confusion and fear that began to affect Hitler's forces as they advanced deeper into the Soviet Union in 1941. The Germans were totally unprepared for either the strength of the Red Army's recovery from early defeats or the chilling ferocity of the Russian winter.

The Japanese attacked Pearl Harbor on December 7, 1941, a day which President Roosevelt said "will live in infamy." The raid crippled the U.S. Pacific Fleet, but it brought the United States into the war and eventually helped bring about the defeat of Hitler's Third Reich.

> The Hitlerites are deprived of honor and conscience, and they have the morals of beasts.
> —JOSEPH STALIN

Hitler to call a retreat. But now the Führer was beyond reason. He felt that his generals had failed him and, out of frustration and sheer suicidal spite, he told them to stand and fight regardless.

In December the Red Army launched its first major counteroffensive, inflicting terrible casualties on the Germans, who had no choice but to sacrifice their lives. More than 1 million Russians fell in the first 10 weeks of battle, and nearly half that number of Germans. Hitler remained inflexible. Stay and fight, he ordered. Fight till you drop. And drop they did, by the thousands.

By the end of 1941 the war held little promise of success for Hitler, but he was the last to recognize the fact. A man obsessed, he lived for his vision of the war, and withdrew further and further from the real world.

In December 1941 his hopes for victory received another major blow. Japanese naval aircraft attacked the United States Pacific Fleet at Pearl Harbor, in Hawaii, and the isolationist government of America was forced to enter the war. President Roosevelt declared war on Japan, an act which led Germany and Italy, Japan's allies, to declare war on the United States. Although Roosevelt had promised to keep his country out of war, he was now impelled to declare every American "a partner in the most tremendous undertaking in our national history." America's war in the Pacific with Japan also meant war in Europe with Hitler and Mussolini.

Confronted with a new, powerful enemy across the Atlantic—an enemy on whose neutrality he had depended—Hitler saw the specter of defeat looming closer. The next year, 1942, brought not only further setbacks in the Soviet Union but also a severe and irrecoverable reverse in North Africa, where Erwin Rommel, one of Hitler's most able generals, had repeatedly fought the British to a standstill. By September of that year, however, British forces under General Bernard Montgomery and units of the Free French were preparing to deliver a final blow to Rommel—and again Hitler sent orders not to retreat. On October 23, 1942, a thousand-gun bombardment by British artillery announced the commencement of the Battle of Alamein. Six weeks later Montgomery's Eighth Army had completely destroyed Rommel's once seemingly invincible Afrika Korps. The defeat in North Africa meant yet another staggering blow to Hitler's prospects.

On November 22, 1942, Soviet forces surrounded the German Sixth Army at Stalingrad. The subsequent siege lasted 10 weeks and the fighting was so fierce that of the 250,000 German troops originally trapped in the encirclement, only 91,000 were left alive when Field Marshal Friedrich von Paulus agreed to a surrender on January 31, 1943.

The fortunes of war continued to vary, but everyone could see that the end was in sight. In July 1943 the Allies mounted a successful invasion of Sicily, off the southern coast of Italy. The Italians—Germany's only real allies—had by now become thoroughly sick of a war they had never wanted, and they had begun to see Mussolini for the opportun-

News of Hitler's death is greeted with cheers on May 1, 1945, by New Yorkers waving slightly inaccurate newspaper headlines. Hitler had indeed died, but not in battle. The day before, he and Eva Braun, his bride of one day, had killed themselves in a Berlin bunker.

American president Franklin Roosevelt (1882-1945) and British prime minister Winston Churchill (1874-1965) meet in Casablanca, Morocco, to discuss Allied strategy. On January 24, 1943—exactly one week before the German defeat at Stalingrad—the two leaders announced that they would accept nothing less than Nazi Germany's unconditional surrender.

Soldiers of the U.S. Third Division await action in Italy following the historic Allied landing in Normandy, France, on D-Day—June 6, 1944. The noose around the Third Reich was growing increasingly tight.

ist he was. He had promised them an empire, they realized, and led them to nothing but death and defeat.

Mussolini inspired none of the mindless, fanatic loyalty Hitler enjoyed. On July 24, 1943, Italy's Fascist Grand Council berated their leader for his conduct of the war, demanded his resignation, and called for a return to constitutional monarchy. On the following day Mussolini tendered his resignation to Victor Emmanuel III, the king whom he and his Blackshirts had successfully intimidated 21 years earlier. As Mussolini left the monarch's villa he was arrested by militiamen acting on the orders of Marshal Pietro Badoglio, the new head of government. Badoglio wasted no time in opening surrender negotiations. Italy signed an armistice with the Allies on September 3, 1943, the same day that General Montgomery's Eighth Army landed on the Italian mainland. This landing was a prelude to the main invasion, which began a few days later when the Anglo-American Fifth Army went ashore in the Gulf of Salerno, near Naples.

On September 12 German commandos rescued Mussolini and took him to Hitler's headquarters in East Prussia. Following a short and bitter conference, the hapless Duce, at Hitler's insistence, announced that he would return to Italy and take charge of Fascism in that country. Sheltered from the Allies and his own people by the German armies in Italy, his regime was to last another 18 months. Hitler, who had once ruled Europe, found himself alone and fighting losing battles on two fronts.

By now many of his own senior military and political aides had begun to become disillusioned, and there was occasional talk of surrender. Hitler refused even to discuss it. From the very beginning he had often said he would go down fighting, regardless of the numbers of people that might fall with him. It was a philosophy of desperation, presenting a very special problem to those members of his entourage who did not share it. Since Hitler still commanded so much support and blind obedience within the party, the army, and the general population, there was no way successfully to oppose him other than to kill him. On July 20, 1944, some of his highest-ranking generals tried to do just that.

Following the massive Allied invasion of France in June 1944, many of the generals opposed to Hitler decided that the time had come to eliminate the Führer. There could be no negotiation with the western Allies (Britain and the United States) while Hitler remained alive, and many of the general staff believed that while the war was going badly for Germany on all three fronts—western, eastern, and Italian—a post-Hitler government might be able to sue for a separate peace on the western front and then persuade Britain and the United States to exert diplomatic pressure on the Soviet Union, and thus stop the fighting on the eastern front. The generals realized that Germany had lost the war.

The bomb planted in the conference room at Hitler's headquarters in East Prussia maimed several of those present but failed to achieve the conspirators' main objective. Hitler emerged from the debris with his trousers in shreds and his heart set on revenge.

The luck that had preserved him from the attempt on his life was nowhere in evidence on the battlefield. By the end of September 1944 the Red Army had already taken Finland and the Balkans, and by February 1945 Soviet forces were at the doors of Germany itself.

Hitler continued to direct the war from a bomb shelter in Berlin. He stormed around the bunker—the shelter he now called home—raging against the "traitors" who had betrayed him—generals like von Paulus and useless allies like Mussolini.

Toward the end, he developed a nervous tremor in his left arm and leg. He talked endlessly, and often it was impossible to follow what he said. Göring regularly fell asleep in his company.

His cruelties during his last weeks as chancellor of the Reich knew no bounds. The attempt on his life had made him distrustful of the army, and he raged for hours on the increasingly familiar theme of betrayal. Movies were made of the slow, horrible

Hitler appears charmed by a little girl in this picture, which was found in Eva Braun's photograph album six months after the couple's death. The child, identified only as "Uschi," was thought by some historians to be the daughter of the dictator and his mistress.

Prisoners in Dachau concentration camp—many of them children—give a rousing welcome to their rescuers, troops of the U.S. Seventh Army, in May 1945. Had the Allied advance into Germany been delayed, most of these inmates would have died in the camp's gas chambers.

Nothing is spared to me. No allegiances are kept, no honor lived up to, no disappointment that I have not had, no betrayal that I have not experienced.... Nothing remains. Every wrong has already been done me.

—ADOLF HITLER
speaking in 1945,
shortly before his death

deaths of the conspirators, some of whom were hung on meat hooks and strangled with piano wire. Hitler and Goebbels watched these visual records of the Führer's taste for extreme cruelty as Germany collapsed around them.

The astonishing thing about these last days was not that the half-crazed Führer should begin to break down completely under so much pressure. He had never been truly rational to begin with, and his deterioration at the end was perfectly understandable. What is hard to fathom as we look back on those days is the hold he continued to have on most of those around him. Few people ever defied him, from the lowliest soldier to the proudest field marshal—they simply went on taking suicidal orders and carrying them out to the best of their abilities.

The public remained behind him as loyally as the army. The German people were so mesmerized by this grotesque little Austrian that they were willing to accept certain death rather than act against him.

On April 12, 1945, the news reached Germany that America's President Franklin D. Roosevelt had died. It was very encouraging to the now almost crippled Hitler—the first good news he had heard for weeks.

On April 29, however, other, more threatening news reached the Führer. His old ally Mussolini had been caught, trying to escape in disguise, by anti-fascist Italian partisans and shot. The bullet-riddled bodies of the fallen dictator and his mistress Clara Petacci were hung by the heels like sides of pork for the public to abuse.

It was the last major blow to Hitler's hopes. Only two more days remained to him. His thousand-year Reich had proven the shortest Reich of all. After just 12 years it had disintegrated completely.

Göring, who now considered himself Hitler's heir, was under the illusion that he might be able to negotiate with the Allies when they reached Berlin. Himmler had much the same idea, thinking perhaps that the Americans and the British might overlook the mass murder of European Jewry and the Soviets might forget their 20 million civilian and military casualties.

While Hitler's leading lackeys thus demonstrated that they were as mad as the Führer himself, Eva Braun proved her own devotion to the dictator by disobeying his orders and joining him in the bunker. Even in his final agony of self-pity, Hitler was able to recognize the simple affections of this wretched girl he had ignored for so long. No other person had remained so loyal to him. "Poor, poor, Adolf," his mistress whined, "deserted by everyone, betrayed by all."

In a rare display of humanity, Hitler decided to reward the faithful Eva. In the early morning of April 29, nine days after his 56th birthday, he married her.

That day was a busy one for the groom. He dictated his will, accused most of his closest associates of treason, and named his appointees to the government that would take office upon his death.

On April 30 Hitler killed his dog and put a bullet through his own brain. His bride took poison beside him on the sofa. Fearful of having his body abused like his old idol Mussolini, he left instructions that he and Eva were to be burned. No one knows to this day what became of the ashes.

As he had predicted, most of his chief henchmen tried to save their own skins at the end. Some ran, some hid, some offered deals. Apparently few got away. It is known, however, that many other Nazi officials took new identities and escaped to or are still living in South America, the United States, and France. Only the faithful Dr. Goebbels remained loyal to the end. On May 1, after performing his last official service by reporting that Hitler had died leading troops into battle, Joseph Goebbels and his wife calmly administered a cyanide capsule to each of their six little children and killed themselves. On May 7, 1945, German representatives signed the instruments of surrender at Allied headquarters in the French city of Rheims. The war in Europe was over.

The following year the Allies tried all the major

> *I assure you, we are all appalled by all these persecutions and atrocities. It is simply not typically German! Can you imagine that I could kill anyone? Tell me honestly, do any of us look like murderers?*
> —JOACHIM VON RIBBENTROP
> former foreign minister of Nazi Germany, speaking at his trial

Hermann Göring enters the war-crimes courtroom in Nuremberg, Germany, in late 1945. Defiant to the end, he was the only defendant to praise Hitler's conduct of the war. Sentenced to death, he escaped the hangman by committing suicide with poison.

> *I had been brought up by my parents to be respectful and obedient toward all grown-up people, and especially the elderly, regardless of their social status.... It was constantly impressed upon me ... that I must obey promptly the wishes and commands of my parents, teachers, and priests, etc., and indeed of all grown-up people.... Whatever they said was always right.... From my earliest youth I was brought up with a strong awareness of duty.*
>
> —RUDOLF HÖSS
> concentration camp commandant

> *From our entire training, the thought of refusing an order just did not enter one's head, regardless of what kind of order it was.*
>
> —RUDOLF HÖSS
> concentration camp commandant

Nazi figures they could catch in a special court for war criminals. Papen, the silky aristocrat who had been Hitler's vice-chancellor, managed to talk his way out of his involvement with the regime. Two others were acquitted and eight defendants received long prison sentences. Himmler swallowed poison before they could try him, and Göring—furious because he was sentenced to be hanged instead of shot, as a soldier should be executed—took poison after he was convicted. Ten others went to the gallows, Ribbentrop leading the gloomy parade.

From time to time other leading Nazis have been uncovered—Eichmann, the methodical administrator of the Final Solution, was tracked down in Argentina years later—but the world has not yet been satisfied. A few isolated punishments hardly balance the scales. The death camps have been pulled down, the innumerable war dead buried, the devastated lands restored. Years have passed, and the bodies of villains and victims alike have returned to dust. And yet the world stands bewildered and helpless before the memory of those years. Generations pass, but the image remains before us.

The Nazi era remains the subject of close study and analysis. New facts come to light every year and allow for ever-increasing accuracy in seeking the root causes of the Nazi madness. Many people imagine that Hitler's life and deeds are to be seen as a monstrous freak of history and that such a situation could never be repeated. Yet this view tends to overlook the tragic fact that militarism, nationalism, genocidal hatred, racism, and murderous tyranny have not been buried forever beneath the ruins of Berlin.

Is it not possible that somewhere in the world another Führer or dictator may be coming to power on a wave of desperate and fanatical patriotism? The silent figure of Adolf Hitler, the embittered maniac standing at the heart of Europe's convulsions, may well be history's greatest example of the dark side of leadership, but there is no darkness so great that it cannot be illuminated.

Chronology

April 20, 1889	Born Adolf Hitler, in Braunau, Austria
Sept. 1907	Moves to Vienna
Sept. 1908	Fails to gain admission to Vienna Academy of Fine Arts
May 24, 1913	Moves to Munich, Germany
Aug. 1, 1914	German declaration of war on Russia signals outbreak of World War I
Aug. 16, 1914	Hitler joins 16th Bavarian Reserve Infantry Regiment
Nov. 11, 1918	Armistice ends World War I
1919	Hitler joins Reichswehr political intelligence bureau and becomes member of German Workers party
1920	German Workers party renamed National Socialist German Workers party (NSDAP)
Nov. 11, 1923	Hitler arrested for involvement in Beer Hall Putsch
Dec. 20, 1924	Released from prison (where he has written most of *Mein Kampf*) on parole
May 22, 1926	Appointed supreme leader of NSDAP Assumes responsibility for party policy and ideology
1930	NSDAP makes massive gains in national elections, emerging as second largest party *Mein Kampf* becomes a best-seller
Jan. 30, 1933	Hitler appointed chancellor by President Hindenburg
Aug. 1934	Declares himself Führer, combines chancellorship and presidency
Sept. 1934	Orders massive increase in military spending
March 7, 1936	Germany effects remilitarization of Rhineland
March 29, 1936	Hitler's policies approved by 98.8% of German electorate
Oct. 1936	Hitler concludes alliance with fascist Italy
1938	Incorporates Austria and Czechoslovakia into Third Reich
Sept. 1, 1939	German invasion of Poland signals outbreak of World War II
1940	German forces invade Norway, Denmark, Belgium, Luxembourg, the Netherlands, and France
June 22, 1941	German forces invade the Soviet Union
Dec. 7, 1941	Japanese attack on American naval base in Hawaii brings United States into the war
Jan. 31, 1943	Surrender of German Sixth Army at Stalingrad destroys Hitler's hopes of victory in Soviet Union
Sept. 7, 1943	Italian surrender announced
June 6, 1944	Allied forces invade German-occupied France Hitler's armies now fighting on three fronts
July 20, 1944	Hitler narrowly escapes assassination by dissident army officers
Dec. 1944	Failure of last major German offensive on western front
April 30, 1945	Hitler commits suicide as Soviet armies enter Berlin
May 7, 1945	Germany surrenders unconditionally

Further Reading

Bullock, Alan. *Hitler: A Study in Tyranny.* New York: Harper & Row, 1962.

Carr, William. *Hitler: A Study in Personality and Politics.* New York: St. Martin's Press, 1979.

Fest, Joachim C. *Hitler.* New York: Harcourt,Brace,Jovanovich, 1974.

Heiden, Konrad. *Hitler: A Biography.* New York: Alfred A. Knopf, 1936.

Herzstein, Robert. *Adolf Hitler and the German Trauma: 1913-1945.* New York: Putnam, 1974.

Hitler, Adolf. *Mein Kampf.* Boston: Houghton Mifflin, 1943.

Jetzinger, Franz. *Hitler's Youth.* Westport, Conn.: Greenwood Press, 1976.

Langer, Walter C. *The Mind of Adolf Hitler.* New York: New American Library, 1973.

Maser, Werner. *Hitler: Legend, Myth, and Reality.* New York: Harper & Row, 1973.

Shirer, William L. *The Rise and Fall of the Third Reich.* New York: Simon & Schuster, 1960.

Speer, Albert. *Inside the Third Reich.* New York: Macmillan, 1970.

Stein, George. *Hitler.* Englewood Cliffs, N.J.: Prentice Hall, 1968.

Stone, Norman. *Hitler.* Boston: Little,Brown, 1980.

Toland, John. *Adolf Hitler.* New York: Doubleday, 1976.

Trevor-Roper, H.R. *The Last Days of Hitler.* New York: Macmillan, 1962.

Index

Dennis Wepman has a graduate degree in linguistics from Columbia University and has written widely on sociology, linguistics, popular culture, and American folklore. He now teaches English at Queens College for the City University of New York. He is the author of *Simón Bolívar* and *Jomo Kenyatta* in the Chelsea House series WORLD LEADERS PAST & PRESENT.

Arthur M. Schlesinger, jr., taught history at Harvard for many years and is currently Albert Schweitzer Professor of the Humanities at City University of New York. He is the author of numerous highly praised works in American history and has twice been awarded the Pulitzer Prize. He served in the White House as special assistant to presidents Kennedy and Johnson.